ALTRUISM

James R. Ozinga

Westport, Connecticut
London

Library of Congress Cataloging-in-Publication Data

Ozinga, James R.
    Altruism / James R. Ozinga.
        p.   cm.
    Includes bibliographical references and index.
    ISBN 0–275–96735–2 (alk. paper)
    1. Altruism.   I. Title.
  BJ1474.O85   1999
    171′.8—dc21   99–22137

British Library Cataloguing in Publication Data is available.

Library of Congress Catalog Card Number: 99–22137
ISBN: 0–275–96735–2

First published in 1999

Praeger Publishers, 88 Post Road West, Westport, CT 06881
An imprint of Greenwood Publishing Group, Inc.
www.praeger.com

Printed in the United States of America

The paper used in this book complies with the
Permanent Paper Standard issued by the National
Information Standards Organization (Z39.48–1984).

10 9 8 7 6 5 4 3 2 1

FOR
SUZANNE OZINGA

MY

SINE QUA NON

Every [person] must decide whether to walk in the light of creative altruism or the darkness of selfishness. This is the judgment. Life's most persistent and urgent question is, what are you doing for others?

Rev. Dr. Martin Luther King Jr.

Contents

Preface

More than thirty years ago I began to teach political philosophy, the story of Western Civilization, and the idea and implementations of communism in various parts of the world to varied groups of university undergraduates. I enjoyed the experience. The data never seemed to wear thin and neither did the students. There were always new faces to speak to and more that I could learn to fill in my knowledge gaps as one element in the chain of development led to another, and the previously unseen connections between things began to appear as clearly as the colors in an old painting when its cleaned. It all became one story of human hopes and dreams and struggles and pain, not just Western either, but a story of Hebrews, Turks, Russians, Arabs, Europeans, and Americans both north and south that make this world both a heaven and a hell.

And this all began to fit together in part because of the education and background I had had in Calvinist Christianity. I was educated in Calvinist parochial schools all the way through seven years of college and seminary that resulted in passing the examination for the Bachelor of Divinity degree. To all this religious indoctrination (e.g., a Christian view of history), church attendance was compulsory at least twice a week, there were weekly catechism classes in which the Heidelburg Catechism was memorized but seldom understood, Sunday School once a week, and prayers, Bible readings, and religious discussions at home. It might be understandable then that by the time I was in my mid-twenties and wanted to leave the career path of a young theologian, Calvinism was beginning to chafe. I discovered that when you took away one of the rational pillars of Calvinism the whole thing fell apart, but by that time the whole Christian religion was gone.

I never did get back to Christianity as a religion, even if I did finally come to my senses about my need for a spiritual life and a firm sense of theism that made sense in my life. This is all very personal and I would not bring it up in print like this for all the world to see except that the chapters that follow in this book may be more understandable with my background in mind. I am not an atheist trying to hurt other's religions, nor bitter about the church and trying to get everyone worshipping under a tree so as to deprive the clergy of the collection plate. None of that even though I believe that Christian churches made a big mistake back in the fourth century when they began to specify orthodoxy and fought to preserve the institution of the church rather than the message. The first action made them intolerant, while the second pulled them away from the people they were supposed to serve.

It took a few decades before I finally figured out a personal spiritual life. I would never have made it had I not had the lovely opportunity of teaching the broad strokes of the past, and seeing how one set of ideas influenced and fit into another over time, and how philosophy and religion seemed to play off each other. I think that as a reader you will be able to tell that I have come to several conclusions about what I am writing, but my conclusions don't have to be yours. I very much want to preserve a toleration of ambiguity, a toleration of different views and ideas, even though I am strongly attached to my own. So if, sometimes, it seems as though I am pushing my own conclusions off on you and you are resistant, please be tolerant of my preachiness.

One of the places in all this where my students normally had a difficult time was in visualizing heaven. Heaven, it seems, is a word like soul—often used but seldom understood. And by the time we figured out the various components of heaven we discovered that we were also describing the secular or empirical futures that Marx, Engels, Lenin, and other spokespeople for a coming Golden Age had envisaged. Or that both Augustine and Hobbes, whom we disliked, had a good deal in common. And that Aristotle was dull.

Another place where student minds focused was on the movement in Karl Marx's historical materialism from one mode of production to another. The stimulus for each new age was supposed to be revolution, a big social revolution, but we couldn't ever find one to correspond to the needed change. And it seemed to my students that the biggest stumbling block to Marx's notions of communism was the inability, so they thought, of selfish individualists in capitalism suddenly to become the sharing collectivists in postrevolutionary socialism.

It never made much sense to dwell on the magic of the socialization of the means of production because no one ever knew how that was to be accomplished. It was simply talked about as though it were understood by all. By the time I was teaching, there were at least two examples of the socialization of the means of production; a total nationalization such as was accomplished for the Soviet Union in 1928, and a partial nationalization that was attempted by the Labour party in Britain after 1945. Neither was very successful in the long run, but successes in the short run kept believers happy for a time.

Nor were my students happy with the awareness that Marx was an environmentalist in the sense that the individual was shaped by the environment. If the new ambience in socialism was *social* then the individual psyche would gradually come to resemble that ambience. Students could accept a partial transition in people's character but not such a total one as Marx envisaged.

It was at this time that I began to consider selfishness seriously. Just how selfish or how altruistic were we in given circumstances? When I was given an opportunity in 1977 to present a paper to an International Conference of Cybernetics and General Systems Theorists in Amsterdam, I jumped at the chance to present a paper on a subject that seemed some distance from political science (supposedly my field) and outside the loop of topics at my usual conferences. It also seemed distant from what I understood about General Systems Theory. Altruism and cybernetics? Why not? My initial paper was so well received that I gave another two years later, and continued doing it, I suppose, because the group continued to applaud, and I continued to derive great pleasure from the research and writing, stimulated both by my interest in altruism and the chosen topic of each conference. Before I knew it, twenty years had passed, and I had given ten fairly unusual papers that dealt with altruism in many different connections.

Because I had so much fun writing them, and because they were so well received by the people who heard them in the first place, I thought that perhaps they might find a small audience in the late 1990s.

Happy reading.

Introduction

Altruism is a word that can excite a strong response from people. To some people the word must be a reminder of their own youth, a time when they had expectations of a kind world or felt that happy endings in books and movies were regularly replicated in real life. Somewhere in the process of growing up, even the romantic individual realizes how unromantic the world can be, how utterly selfish and uncaring people can be and begins to expect others to run away from an accident rather than running toward it to see if help is needed. Some may believe that the word altruism means giving to charity, and the responder immediately lets one know that she gave at the office, thank you. The response in either case is defensive, wary. Or the responder takes the word altruism to mean people receiving something for which they have not worked, or do not merit, as though altruism were an automatic pejorative referring to throwing away money. Others seem to feel that altruism means the sacrifice of themselves to some saintly objective; that if they were expected to be altruistic then they would not resent the driver who cut them off or the lady who stole the empty place in the crowded parking lot. They react aggressively as though the concept of altruism demands an inhuman perfection that they do not nor could ever expect to have. This reaction unfortunately relegates altruism to the perfect future rather than to the present and acts as though selfishness is synonymous with being human and altruism with godliness. For a word that is not used frequently, it certainly creates a reaction; a surprising reaction considering how unattractive its opposite—selfishness—appears.

Altruism in its dictionary meaning simply refers to unselfishness. The positive way of expressing this is unselfish concern for the welfare of others. I have refined this just a bit, so the way the word is used here is as follows: Altruism is behavior benefitting someone else at some cost to oneself, while selfishness is behavior that benefits oneself at some cost to others. If there is no cost there is no altruism, no selfishness. At this point, people often begin to split hairs: They want to know, for example, how great or how small a cost still constitutes cost, beginning to give evidence of a Jesuit education.

Altruism is easier to talk about if one does not worry so much about the precision of the definition: Instead of biting the finger, look where it's pointing. Instead of trying to define God, the point is to try to live a godly life. Altruism is simply doing for others at some cost to oneself, and selfishness is doing for oneself at some cost to others. Please accept this simple definition, do not argue with it. You will be arguing the wrong thing. If altruism is not kept simple, discussion progress is not possible. Altruism is kindness, selfishness is unkindness. Complicate it just a little and all hope dies of making any sense.

So I have tried to keep altruism simple so that I could build mountains on the concept. I look first at its evolutionary source in human conduct, how it seems to be the same thing as what philosophers called *natural law*, and how it flows out of a social instinct. Then the discussions move into what seem like barriers to altruism, whether in the chemistry of the person, outside the person in terms of organized religion or ideology, or outside the person in terms of absolute goals. I then move on to describe unconscious drives noted by Adam Smith that start out as selfishness and end up as altruism, misplaced altruism found in extended family networks and in the old Russian serfdom, and even an unaware connectedness waiting for altruism in eco-altruism. Finally, altruism is visualized as a consumer of sin, as a virtuous activity that counteracts sin, and causes it to disappear.

None of the chapters preach a sermon, but they will push at you to think differently, to consider things differently than you did the day before. And as you read these chapters you may come to agree that altruistic behavior is virtuous behavior, even godly behavior without any religious connotations or involvement. Selfishness, on the other hand, and speaking simply, is on the evil side, the sin side. Selfishness is Socrates' ignorant behavior, the behavior that does not see the connections with the world beyond the physical.

The topic of altruism can, therefore, rapidly segue to a different frame of reference and illumine both itself and the new field in which it has inserted itself. Once the pleasure of this was discovered it was not difficult to find other areas, and before long, the word altruism was tying whole areas of thought together in different and heuristic ways. For example, thinking about altruism raised the issue of whether the religious concept of *sin* was the equivalent of selfishness; whether altruism was helped or harmed by being captured by religious folk, or by being so frequently cast in the mold of some perfect standard or goal. Wasn't altruism always beneficial? Perhaps not if it resulted in more poverty and misery. And so on. Once one's mind opens to possibilities, the subject of altruism is anything but dry.

This book does not exhaust the topic. My wife, Suzanne, is my critic and editor, and often while we are walking on the beach or sitting in a restaurant, headings for other chapters occur to us. And, because of our exposure to this book we are more aware of altruism, although neither of us always is. We try, however, and that's all anyone can do.

Part I

The Source

Where do the human qualities like altruism or selfishness come from? Are they natural to the human or are they imposed from the outside through environmental conditioning and training? If they are from the outside where are they when they are not within a person; lying in some quality bank in the heavens? This line of approach begs more questions than it answers, so why not assume that both altruism and selfishness are natural qualities existing in all humans in varying degrees?

Assuming that they are natural qualities, the question of how they pass from one generation to another can be asked. If one assumes either a creation or an evolution that begins with one male and one female it can be alleged that the qualities came from them in some form of transmission, such as genetic transmission, or as a part of the human instinct, or even as an essence of a moral code somehow inscribed in the physical brain. If one assumes a multiple evolution with a variety of starting points the task is more difficult and messier.

At the present stage of human development, there are no simple answers to these questions of source. Perhaps in another century the human genome will be completely understood, unravelled, and no longer complex. Perhaps people on the street will wear perfumes that block the pheromones from others that might alter their behavior. As of now, however, it all seems mysterious and the temptation to fall back on old, tired explanations is hard to resist. One example of an old and tired explanation is the blending of Aristotle's use of Plato's Form to construct a theory of how humans transmit qualities. Aristotle argued that the growth of an oak tree followed the pattern or form of the tree located within the material of the acorn, the form that actualized into the mature tree. What Aristotle apparently meant as a metaphysical force, something like the soul, realized in the final stage of the growth of a thing was used by Jan Swammerdam and Nicolas Malebranche to refer to physical forms for the entire future. This was the idea of preformation, the notion that all of us existed from the beginning as very very small entities in the womb of Eve based on the assumption that things could become smaller and smaller all the way to infinity. It would be possible, for example, to have an entire nation of small people on the head of a pin. Malebranche wrote that perhaps all the bodies of men and animals born until the end of times were created at the creation of the world, which is to say that the females of the first animals were created containing all the animals of the same species that they have begotten and that are to be begotten in the future.[1] This is a strange idea that suggests that we have all existed fully formed since the beginning of time (Eve).

The chapters that make up Part I, much milder than preformation, provide three speculative but possible ideas about the source of altruism; it is in our genes, or it is a part of our natural law, or a major component of the drive for socialness. Perhaps a bit of all three.

NOTE

1. Clara Pinto-Correia, *The Ovary of Eve: Egg and Sperm and Preformation* (Chicago: University of Chicago Press, 1997), p. 19. Readers with small children or grandchildren may be reminded of the video *Horton Hears a Who* in which very tiny people in trouble were saved by Horton the elephant only to discover even tinier people in need.

Chapter 1

The Genetic Possibility

One of the ways of describing a behavioral characteristic as a permanent part of the human is to claim that it is a part of the genetic heritage, either placed there by a creator or by chance as it evolved along with all the other characteristics of a human that have been developed these past 100,000 years or so. This might be expressed as a gene for altruism carried along with other genes on the prehuman (evolution) and human (creation and/or evolution) chromosomes, a gene responsible for the giving, sharing actions that counter and seek to overcome the selfish and greedy *taking* that characterizes so much of the human story.

There would be no need to refer to genes at all were it not for the fact that both altruism and selfishness appear to be natural rather than artificial components of the human system. When discussing the source, therefore, one has to go back in time. If altruism were something one received from the air or from water or from eating certain vegetables it would be artificial. If it is in one from birth, it is natural.

So, could genes be the answer to the question of source? If one is willing to go back to the beginning of humanness, and is a creationist, one stops regressing at the Garden of Eden. If one has evolution as part of a creation package or as the sole determiner of humans, it is necessary to regress further into the prehumans. To say that ten million years ago a thirty-pound animal named Ramapithecus who lived in trees or on the land, and who did not normally walk upright, or that Lucy, a short female with a small brain and a pronounced V-shaped jaw who walked upright most of the time was a probable ancestor of humans does not say much about altruism or selfishness, although it may say a good deal about paleo-anthropology. About two million years ago, evidence supports bipeds with larger brains who used tools. The resemblance to humans becomes stronger and perhaps altruism was already there.

Certainly, the limbic system in the brain already existed. This group of subcortical structures concerned with emotions and motivation guided these long-ago individuals to appropriate behavior without preceding conscious thought. This activity, normally called *instinctual behavior*, is present in both animals and humans. For example, in laboratory studies, the visual cliffs experiments demonstrated that very young animals will not cross over an area that appears to have a substantial drop off. Similarly, human babies respond more to drawings of human faces than they do to illustrations in which the same lines are assembled randomly. Both of these responses are the result of the limbic system. Are both altruism and selfishness similar instincts that were in place long before the larger brain in our more recent ancestors permitted the development of language and conceptualization? Quite likely, although when this actually began is impossible to determine. The writing left by the ancient Sumerians around 3300 B.C. is still the earliest record of that ability. Since agriculture began around seven thousand years earlier, it appears to have begun without writing although probably not without some form of language. Gatherers and hunters lived for eons before that, so these instincts, if that is what they were, are millions of years old.

This very long evolutionary record should not be discarded because in very early times the record refers to animals who were not humans. There is a boundary of sorts between animals and humans, but it is not that strong a boundary. When differences are overstressed, people imagine that only humans possess rational ability. Carrying that further, some people imagined that homo sapiens were the pinnacle of creation/evolution, shaped in a divine image, and the difference between humans and other animals became unbridgable.

We carried this rationalizing too far, of course, having no idea where to stop. Having no power outside ourselves to check us, we created one, in our rationalizing image and in the process became puppets who imagined that they controlled the puppeteer. We began to treat hypotheses and speculations as truths, as givens, and on these foundations of straw we erected myths and philosophies and ethics, and presumed that the real world operated according to the rules of our minds. This gave us an even greater sense of specialness, suggesting that we could not possibly be related to an animal like Ramapithecus who loosely resembled one of our dogs.

Our tie with the animal world has been there all along in many observable ways. According to Dr. Dorothy Miller,[1] a geneticist at Columbia University College of Physicians and Surgeons, the current evidence indicates that humans, chimps, and gorillas are about equidistant from each other and that all three share a common ancestor some eight to twelve million years ago. Professor Yunis of the University of Minnesota has argued a remarkable similarity between human and chimpanzee genes. Studies show that 99 percent of the genetic material in humans is similar to that found in the chimp.[2] The structure is different, and that is important, but the gene pool is very similar. Note that these studies stress the similarities rather than exploiting the differences so as to project a human uniqueness. It helps to be a biologist, perhaps, in daily contact with intelligent, feeling animals to understand that the similarities may be more important than the differences.

Part of the problem in accepting this is that we are used to thinking about genes as carriers of physical traits such as height, coloring, and the shape of the face. Some genes also carry behavior traits and geneticists are only beginning to understand these. It seems clear that the behavior genes are precoded in general rather than specific terms; that the response pattern to the stimulus of need in another is either altruism or selfishness. This precoded response, moreover, is not unique to humans. It has been around for a long time.

Before moving to examples, however, it is wise to repeat the definitions of the words being used here. *Altruism* is doing something for another at some cost to oneself. *Selfishness* is doing something for oneself at some cost to others. The cost to self or to others may be mild or severe. The altruistic or selfish behaviors are mutually exclusive (e.g., when one is altruistic one is not selfish and vice versa). It is important not to combine the two, even though both behaviors seem to be dichotomies that some philosophers saw as unresolved concepts that could be unified by some sort of metatheorizing. Hegel and Marx, for example, both sought resolution of conflict and valued the conflict as motivating the resolution. The mutually exclusive behaviors are alternative responses to the same stimulus.

To speculate that there is a gene that prompts altruism or selfishness is reasoning backward from behavior to genetic cause, assuming that there is a bit of DNA on the chromosome, which may one day be isolated, that carries both behaviors as potential responses to perceived need in another. Instead of seeing the resolution within the imagined boundary of a rationalized humanness, the resolution is actually within physical human nature. At the same time, another of the boundaries between humans and nonhumans disappears, because the behavior of many nonhuman animals strongly suggests that the gene for altruism–selfishness must be present in the nonhuman population as well. This, in turn, suggests that still another boundary—that between nature and nurture—needs a rethinking and reformulation; not because of a sudden shrinking of the scope of the nurture dimension, but because of the need to better understand the role of the environment in shaping human behavior and also to visualize the significance of the role of nurture in channeling human evolution.

Are humans a cooperating or a competing set of animals? Or is this a false question with the dichotomy more a description of extreme groups rather than human individuals? In attempting to ask this question, does one's answer seem to describe real people rather than ideal "types?" To determine the answer to this last question requires an exploration of all available material in the most careful manner possible.

The background for this question in the nineteenth century was the manner in which the various theories of Charles Darwin were used to justify a rapacious kind of competition or aggression in nature. Darwin had highlighted a struggle for existence in which the prize of survival went to the fittest. Evolution, in this view, was a weeding out process in which the weak and the ill were gradually replaced by the healthy and strong. Those who could not change failed in the face of the adaptive necessity. Darwin did not mean to slight cooperation within the same species, for he also wrote about the importance of sociality and the social instinct in animals that resulted in group well-being and survival. But the phrase, survival of the fittest, proved too handy a slogan for the nineteenth century's search for a rational justification for a very bad distribution of wealth and power. Notions of sociability and cooperation were played down, whereas in Darwin's work they had slightly counterbalanced the struggle side. The group struggle for survival was recast into an individual struggle against the wider world but also against members of one's own species. As the "rational people" in John Locke's state of nature were the property holders, so also did the "fittest" become synonymous with the successful in Social Darwinism. The slogan, survival of the fittest, in the glow of a progressive evolution justified the struggle and the extremely unequal distribution of resources. The slogan that came to mean "woe to the weak" was raised to the level of natural law or religious belief. To challenge this putative science was to classify oneself as a utopian romantic hopelessly lost on the altruistic side. To join it was to endorse parking lots on prime agricultural land as progress.

A different view was held by Prince Peter Alekséyevich Kropotkin in the late nineteenth–early twentieth century. Kropotkin was a graduate of the Corps of Pages in St. Petersburg who became an officer in Siberia where he took part in two geographical expeditions in fairly wild territory. In 1867 he joined the Russian Geographical Society and began publishing scientific papers about what he had seen on his travels. Originally in the 1860s, when he had teamed up with a zoologist named Poliakov, he sought evidence of an ice age further south than previously documented, endeavored to map and chart mountain ranges not well known, and to find evidence to support Darwin's ideas of competition within species. This latter Kropotkin did not find. He instead discovered a survival based on mutual aid within a species that was far more important to survival than was competition. He began at this point, unwisely perhaps, to apply the mutual aid notion from animals to humans, creating an anarchist basis for a new and better society. He came to believe that mutual aid was something that characterized the human past, but which, in the name of progress, we had left behind in favor of artificial forms of social life. These artificial forms stifled the expression of any direct mutual aid and encouraged an indirect socialness exercised through institutions like fire and police departments.

Kropotkin became busy with other things, however, and his ideas probably would not have been published had he not become angry with the contents of an article written by the Social Darwinist Thomas H. Huxley in 1888, called "Struggle for Existence." Kropotkin responded with a series of articles in a journal called *The Nineteenth Century*, under titles such as mutual aid among animals, savages, barbarians, in the medieval city, and amongst ourselves.[3] What irritated him was that the exaggerated emphasis people like Huxley and Herbert Spencer put on competition was in conflict with his own observations of life in Siberia. He did not mean to deny the importance of competition in the survival struggle; but the great emphasis put on the struggle aspects seemed almost a conspiracy to exclude that part of Darwin that played up cooperation. In response, as a corrective, Kropotkin overemphasized cooperation and played down the competition. Earlier, Kropotkin had become an anarchist and these beliefs lent an antipolitical tone to his conclusions. Mutual aid became very important to him and began to underlie everything he wrote from that point on. The more he dealt with it the more he saw in it a feature of great importance for the maintenance of life and the preservation of the human species. The cooperation he saw among animals, he also saw among people, whether primitive or modern, and the motivating force was an instinct for altruism, not an expression of emotional or sentimental feelings. He refused to reduce animal sociability to either love or sympathy because that lowered its generality and importance, he thought, just as human ethics based on love and personal sympathy only narrowed the comprehension of moral feeling. Like a good many other thinkers in the late nineteenth century, Kropotkin was enamored of science and scientific explanation. He was interested in demonstrating the continuing existence of animal and human altruism but he wanted it understood in a scientific, unemotional way. He wrote that it was not "love to my neighbor—whom I often do not know at all—which induces me to seize a pail of water and to rush towards his house when I see it on fire; it is a far wider, even though more vague feeling or instinct of human solidarity and sociability which moves me."[4]

Mutual aid was a natural push toward solidarity, an instinct toward brotherhood and sisterhood rather than a love or sympathy for others. It could not be called love because Kropotkin felt that love was weaker than the instinct for unity that he witnessed. This instinct developed among animals and humans in their long evolution that taught the survival values of cooperation and the joys of social life. Kropotkin questioned why humans are not more aware of this instinct. The answer would be because the circumstances of our present existence—private property, external government, and bureaucratic authority—stand in the way and block our realizing this instinct's existence in any complete sense.

Examples of that mutual aid among animals included wild, free horses forming a ring to ward off wolves; or the wolves hunting in packs and dividing the chase, some forward and others in the rear; or the beetles together laying their eggs in dead mice and then cooperating in burying the mice to facilitate the birth of the next beetle generation, and so forth. His human examples were things like mothers' clubs, service clubs, crisis emergency committees, or, in medieval times, guild structures. Human instincts to cooperate meaningfully, Kropotkin felt, were largely destroyed by the imposition on the localized society of a strong national government. (Remember his hatred of government.) This imposition resulted in narrow individualism on one side, while the state absorbed all of the social functions on the other side. The individualism, moreover, carried with it an expectation for a lower level of social functioning in the individual. As individual obligations toward the state grew, the citizens' obligations to each other were reduced proportionally. This led people to believe that they not only could but should seek their individual happiness in total disregard for the happiness of others. The only question was whether it is legal not whether it is moral. For example, a person no longer had to worry about helping when a neighbor's house was on fire, one simply called the state agency, the fire department. Someone being robbed or raped? Call the police, or assume that someone else will call them because one does not wish to become personally involved. In these instances the social instinct has been repressed and with enough practice one can forget that a social instinct to help, to cooperate, to feel joint responsibility ever existed at all. These attitudes led to the generally accepted notion that the cooperative onus was taken off individuals and given to the abstraction known as the state. Such ideas led Kropotkin to work for the destruction of governments so as to bring social responsibility back to the people so that in turn the deeply rooted instincts of mutual assistance would again be able to flower.

The idea that altruistic genes, as well as selfish ones, evolved with humans is speculation, of course, but it is based on actual behavior like Kropotkin's horses in Siberia. Nonetheless, anyone who claims to be able to speak *ex cathedra* on genes and animal or human behavior is probably a candidate for supervised retirement. This is a field so complicated that mapping out the human genome by 2005, the goal of several teams of geneticists, is by no means certain. The genome is the complex set of instructions contained in the nucleus of every cell on twenty-three pairs of chromosomes. Already people have begun interpreting what has been mapped. This is called post-genomics, or perhaps bioinformatics or computational biology but it can be just as short-sighted and wrong as the mind of the average interpreter. These hereditary instructions are contained in genes that ride on chromosomes that are made up of long strands of deoxyribonucleic acid (DNA). Those instructions are written in a four-letter code using A, G, C, and T. Figuring out what each instruction may mean to the human (or animal) is extremely difficult.[5] So writing or speaking as though all the answers were in is just not honest. But guessing is always permissible and often fun.

Edward O. Wilson, in his book *On Human Nature*, suggested that genes were unlikely to prescribe particular forms of behavior.

> The behavior genes more probably influence the range of the form and intensity of emotional responses, the thresholds of arousals, the readiness to learn certain stimuli as opposed to others, and the pattern of sensitivity to additional environmental factors that point to cultural evolution in one direction as opposed to another.[6]

If humans share genes with other animals, and it is clear that we do, we also share the same gene pool of the early human ancestors whom Richard Leakey described as gatherers and hunters. Indeed, we are not biologically different from early humans before the development of language and rational thought in the neo-cortex. In other words, our behavioral genes were operating before we became wired for the complex internal communication we now call thinking. Altruism and selfishness (as well as other behaviors) are thus unthinking responses to need, instinctual behavior that seems to have little connection with moral education or with external commands that attempt to place an "ought" where the "is" is already functioning, perhaps at a lower level.

Consider the hypothetical example of driving down the highway and seeing someone in need alongside the road. Do you stop to help? Drive on? Debate on who your neighbor is? You are genetically driven to respond either altruistically or selfishly. The decision is made instantly. If there is sufficient time before passing the needy person, one's neo-cortex can override the limbic decision, and in this instance the moral upbringing that commanded altruism as a good or selfishness as an always safe course to follow may sway the earlier instinctive response. Normally, there is not this much time, and this may be a very good thing; the neo-cortex override can prompt conduct that may be quite unwise in a survival sense.

This suggests that moral codes, systems of ethics, entire philosophies of life are little more than rationalizations that have less to do with human behavior than was thought. The explanation for the failure of thousands of years of preaching then is not the sinfulness of the hearer, but the irrelevance of the sermon. The likely result of preaching is guilt, not altered behavior.

And even if one is reluctant to move from animal to human behavior the analogies are compelling. Both competitive and cooperative genes seem to drive human conduct. They are not necessarily in balance in one person, nor are they in balance, necessarily, in the whole society. The early hunters and gatherers appeared to have strong cooperative drives. Once private property and settled agriculture are introduced, the competitive side of the balance becomes stronger. This would be an environmental seduction of one or the other side of the genetic inheritance, as, for example, the gathering and hunting societies compared with the societies of autonomous individuals preferred by Social Darwinists. Most of history presents less clear examples than this, suggesting that most of the time the two inheritances are in an uneasy sort of balance and conditioned by the environment. Edward O. Wilson wrote in 1975 that although humans have a genetic tendency to aggress, to do so on a wide scale with nuclear weapons would be global suicide.[7] Similarly, to assist someone in need on the expressway late at night might be unwise for even the most altruistic person. The environment or ambience of the proposed action is significant in determining the character of the action.

Also compelling is the analogy that suggests that a self-sacrificing sort of altruism, the soldier who throws himself on the live grenade, is rare when it is not nepotism and is usually rewarded with a high-level medal or great prestige. Michael Grant suggested that this is the kind of altruism Gospel writers alleged about Jesus, who evidently felt that his martyrdom would assist the already begun inauguration of the kingdom of God.[8] Oddly enough, those who believe that this sacrifice was for the entire world would thus have a very high-level example of altruism, whereas those believing in predestination might argue for nepotism; Jesus would be dying only for the family of believers, or what Garritt Hardin might call the "germ line." Often, human altruism is called nepotism because it is so clearly for the germ line, that is, saving one's own children from a burning house. Such thinking frequently seems to be a deliberate effort to deprive altruism of much of its merit; the behavior is given a selfish motive. Such thinkers forget that most occasions of altruism will benefit one's family because one is usually surrounded by family.

There are also those who wish to deny the significance of altruism by calling it reciprocal altruism.[9] Someone sees a fire beginning to burn in a house; not a neighbor's house, just a house. The person stops to alert the family living there and may even help put out the fire. Robert Trivers suggested that the motivation is still selfish—if the situation were reversed one would hope that others would act in a similar fashion, creating sort of a savings account from which one could later draw. This is a silly rendering of "do unto others" because the slogan reads treat others as you would like to be treated not so that you will later be treated likewise. Reciprocal altruism is simply another way in which the significance of human sharing behavior is denigrated. This is discussed again in Chapter 3.

People are generally amazed when they discover that St. Francis was correct when he said that "It is in giving that I receive." It is one of the great joys of giving that so much seems to come back. But does one give so that the joy of receiving can take place? Is receiving then the motivation of giving?

Trying to find a selfish motive and implying that altruism would not exist without that motive denies the loving, caring character of altruism and turns it into its opposite.

The same thing can happen to the concept of human love. Because the verb has been idealized or romanticized to the point of silliness, there is a tendency to pull it down into the "real world." In so doing one can make even love selfish. In this sense, loving is a reciprocal satisfaction of need, a form of Triver's reciprocal altruism in which the love needs of the recipient are satisfied by the giver so that the similar needs of the giver may in turn be filled. One might even describe a monitored feedback loop that permits one to sense when insufficient loving is returning from the lovee, causing a lessening of the lover's efforts. Even the accounts in the Bible about the love of God can be seen in this light. The verses that describe the covenant relationship of God with her people, for example, are prefaced with interesting words that may influence the reader's perception of love or of that God. When Abram was ninety years old and nine, the Bible says, the Lord appeared to Abram, and said unto him, I am the Almighty God; walk before me and be thou perfect, and I will make my covenant between me and thee, and will multiply thee exceedingly (Genesis 17:1–2). This sounds reciprocal. So does the Gospel of John that describes a divine loving that encompasses the world and yet can be restricted nearly immediately. For God so loved the world, it says, that he gave his only begotten Son, *that* whosoever believeth in him should not perish but have everlasting life. (John 3:16; Italics added)

This might argue that unconditional love is impossible, that all love is conditional or reciprocal, depending on some activity by the lovee to keep the love flowing. Furthermore, it would be argued, that this is true whether one is speaking of humans in general, mothers in particular, or even deities. But those that maintain this hard doctrine must never have seen unconditional love, never witnessed a wife's love for an erring husband that defies any rational explanation, a mother or father's love for a child that exists miles above reciprocity, or a love for God clearly independent of the unfolding of God's will. Reciprocal loving and reciprocal altruism indeed exist. But to argue that this is all there is to loving or altruism is, sadly, to miss one of the most important points of life.

But it would also be most unwise to assume that conditional loving or reciprocal altruism has no place, nor that it should be either ignored or discouraged as not quite living up to the mark. People do this when they, in happy ignorance, play with the levels of love, assigning Greek words to the levels, and assuming that the only really good kind of loving is the top level: the *Agape* sort of love that is unconditional and reserved for God alone. Just as the "selfish people" seem to want all altruism to be selfishly motivated, so the *Agape* people seem, by their emphasis, to destroy the importance of loving below the top level. Reciprocity is significant both in loving and in altruism, perhaps, but it is not the most important part.

To argue that altruism is either nepotism or reciprocal is the argument of small minds who conceive of the human as a selfish, grasping individual out only or basically for her or himself. If one assumes that a person has both selfish and altruistic genetic drives, it does not mean that one side needs stressing to the exclusion of the other. Aggressive genes do not have to mean constant, rapacious competition with no regard for those on whom one steps. Altruistic genes do not have to imply the sort of unlimited socialness that Kropotkin described. Nor does Garritt Hardin need to assume that human altruism is only nepotism. These problems are caused by dealing in extremes or absolutes that permit strawmen to be set up only to allow them to be knocked down again.

In Christianity, for example, Christ's second summary commandment is to love ones's neighbor as oneself. When one attempts to operationalize the word neighbor an answer often given is anyone in need. In the Galilee of 30 A.D. this answer worked well, but nearly two thousand years later the scope of the needy has widened well beyond physical proximity. The love that is being described, a giving sort of feeling, should be extended to all areas of the world where there is need, whether that need is human or non-human. Difficult as this is to contemplate, with an operationalization that seems impossible, it is still what has to be done. However, Hardin demonstrated that implementating such a loving could have very undesirable consequences.[10] Unwise assistance, harmful altruism in fact, solves a short term problem at the expense of the future. Hardin.pointed out that the growth of populations beyond the carrying capacity of their territory, with very little to trade, no place to migrate, little power to seize other's goods, and few rich areas left to give without strings all contribute to a decidedly dangerous world. This leads some to conclude that the problem is helping those others and concluding that the only people who can be helped are those in close proximity.

Reciprocity or reciprocal altruism needs to be properly understood with respect to the world surrounding humans as well. The world's ecosystem includes humans as a functioning part that needs to be aware of the human impact on the whole. We are a part of the system, and when we abuse the system, ignore the feedback potential, the system is capable of striking back. Polluted water and soil sickens our food, polluted air our lungs; and as the whole sickens the quality of life declines for every living thing. Altruism should be global, regional, and local. One of the world's silliest activities is a meeting in a church basement to do something about hunger in the Congo when there is abundant evidence of hunger in the neighborhood where the meeting takes place.

Hardin, writing in 1977, achieved more praise than he should have for writing about the importance of selfishness. But he did have a point worth making. He wrote that although there were thousands who would line up to praise generosity compared to the few who have any kind words at all to say about selfishness.

> Yet biology clearly tells us that survival requires a respect for carrying capacity, and points to the utility of territorial behavior in protecting the environment and ensuring the survival of populations. Surely posterity matters. Surely there is something to be said for selfishness."[11]

What is desirable is not to throw the clean baby out with the dirty bath water. Selfishness may be important, but it is not enough. Concern for one's own germ line needs to take others into account both because of the possible importance of those others to one's own germ line and also because cooperation with others is part of what being human is all about. The ethic of the future can derive from both genetic drives that sometimes will appear selfish and sometimes altruistic. Victor Ferkiss described the characteristics of a philosophy suitable for the next century: It would be naturalistic, seeing the human as an integral part of nature; it would be holistic in the sense of understanding the need to balance subsystems without losing awareness of either system or subsystem; and it would be immanentistic—seeing the ethic coming not from the outside, but from within—from the genetic inheritance from the past.[12]

Altruism is an instinct for survival that may be in our genes—an internal force for goodness in everyone that begins with birth.

NOTES

1. Dorothy Miller, remarks in *The New York Times*, July 8, 1980, p 5c.

2. Dr. Jorge J. Yunis, Jeffry R. Sawyer, and Dr. Kelly Dunham whose article in *Science* was excerpted by *The New York Times*, July 8, 1980, 1c.

3. Peter Kropotkin, *Mutual Aid: A Factor in Evolution* (London: William Heinmann, 1915).

4. Ibid., pp. 5–6.

5. For more detailed information on recent efforts to decode the basis of life see Nicholas Wade, "The Struggle to Decipher Human Genes," *The New York Times*, March 10, 1998, pp. B9–10.

6. Edward O. Wilson, *On Human Nature* (Cambridge, MA: Harvard University Press, 1978), p. 45.

7. Edward O. Wilson, "Human Decency is Animal," *The New York Times Magazine*, October 12, 1975, pp. 39ff.

8. Michael Grant, *Jesus, An Historian's Review of the Gospels* (New York: Charles Scribner's Sons, 1977).

9. Robert Trivers, "The Evolution of Reciprocal Altruism," *Quarterly Review of Biology, 1971*, Vol. 46, pp. 35–57.

10. Garrett Hardin, "The Tragedy of the Commons," *Science*, vol. 162, December 1968, pp. 1243–1248.

11. Garrett Hardin, "Ethical Implications of Carrying Capacity," in Hardin and Baden, eds., *Managing the Commons* (San Francisco, CA: Freeman, 1977).

12. Victor Ferkiss, *The Future of Technological Civilization* (New York: Braziller, 1974).

Chapter 2

Altruism as Natural Law

Thoughts of a genetic evolution of altruism and selfishness at least dealt with a physical substance—a gene on a chromosome—that might (or might not) be identified in the future. The subject here is a different sort of evolution of altruism, sort of a metaphysical common denominator that identifies the animal as human. This is the idea of natural law; held by the ancients to be synonymous with altruism, referring to an innate moral law somehow etched or engraved on every human consciousness. This law of human conduct is a natural and expected possession of every person, a part of the human nature, and a corrective for uncivil behavior. In other words, people writing about natural law refer to the same human characteristic, altruism, as did Kropotkin, Wilson, and Trivers. These references to natural law, or altruism, are scattered over time, are brief and poorly connected, but all are views of moral principles that have evolved in human consciousness and assisted human survival by promoting civil behavior.

Aristotle called natural law the universal law that was everywhere the same, which provided the universal justice or lawfulness reflected in the particular justice that he separated into distributive and remedial justice. That was his way of describing what might superficially be called common sense, a common moral sense, because the exercise of natural law was an activity of the rational part of the soul common to every human, or a seed of divinity or a spark from the fire called God according to Stoics. Later Stoics took this concept further. Believing that reason was Logos, the animating fire of universal life, they made a mistake similar to George Hegel's two thousand years later: They abstracted human reason and treated it as deity to the world, a guide to the world as Plato's individual reason was the guide to the person. Cicero wrote that true law was right reason conformable to nature, or making your subjective rationality conform to objective reason, and it was universal, unchangeable, and eternal. Its commands urge us to duty; its prohibitions

restrain us from evil. And he who does not obey it flies from himself and
does violence to the very nature of man.[1]

This law was embedded in our consciousness and it integrated the
natural world of nature outside of people with human nature. Moreover, this
integration, this oneness with nature was ethical in the sense that natural law
provided a sense of social responsibility. Natural law expressed the unity and
the oneness that Hegel tried to prove logically. Human universality and unity
were assumed because of the similarity of natural law around the world rather
than because Reason was God, a Hegelian mistake highlighted by Feuerbach
in 1843.[2] Cicero argued that the content of that natural law was the confirmation and establishment in the human mind that rationality was implanted in
nature and that the rationality in nature could be understood as altruism. "It
follows then, that nature made us just that we might share our goods with each
other and supply each other's wants."[3]

This altruism, Cicero wrote, was based on a natural sympathy rather
than on positive or civil laws. If nature does not ratify law, he wrote, then all
the virtues may lose their sway. What becomes of generosity, patriotism, or
friendship? Where shall the desire of benefiting our neighbors, or the gratitude
that acknowledges kindness, be able to exist at all? For, all these virtues
proceed, he wrote, from our natural inclination to love mankind. And this
love is the true basis of justice, and without this not only the mutual charities
of men, but the religious services of the Gods, would be at an end; for these
are preserved, he wrote, rather by the natural sympathy that subsists between
divine and human beings, than by mere fear and timidity.[4]

What flows out of natural law is love for others that results in
generosity, patriotism, friendship, giving help to others, and expressing
gratitude for kindnesses received. Mayerhoff made this point decades ago:

> I do not try to help the other grow in order to
> actualize myself, but by helping the other grow
> I do actualize myself.[5] I can only fulfill myself
> by serving someone or something apart from
> myself, and if I am unable to care for anyone or
> anything separate from me, I am unable to care
> for myself.[6]

Human sociability derives from the natural inclination to love others. The
basis of all virtue was not something from the outside of the individual but
from inside, a part of his or her personal makeup, etched on human consciousness in some way from the beginning.

This natural drive to sociability is the moral law St. Thomas imagined
discoverable by reason. It was, in his words, the rational creature's participa-
tion in the eternal or highest law. Natural law to St. Thomas was people's
moral reason; the extension of a spiritual principle that transcended nature.[7]

This made the defining characteristic of humans the moral reason that bound them rather than the sin (selfishness) that separates them from each other and from God. St. Thomas, even though he lost his way when trying to demonstrate the deity through reason, was signally significant when he saw natural law or moral reason as the socially unifying principle linked to the eternal law; unifying spirit and nature and giving human reason its spiritual dimension.

The Christian anthropomorphizing of the god concept, however, included a denial of soul to nonhuman nature, necessitating a separation between human and external nature so as to justify treating externalized nature as a servant to human capriciousness. Natural law was narrowed without changing its content. Once begun, the narrowing continued. John Locke, for example, narrowed the concept even further despite using words that indicated a wide application. The law of nature stands, he wrote, "as an eternal rule to all men, legislators as well as others, and the fundamental law of nature being preservation of mankind, no human sanction can be good or valid against it."[8] This preservation of social justice was built on preserving the rights of labor, which meant the rights of private property. It is like saying that something is for "the people" when you do not mean all people. The all-inclusive appearance is illusory. Property is protected by not permitting its just distribution or use. William Bluhm noted that Locke's frequent mentions of charity meant love for one's fellow human in a general sense, not helping the poor as a special instance of such love.[9]

This narrowing of the scope of natural law's content moved the perspective from the collective all-inclusiveness of human and nonhuman nature to the human distinct from the nonhuman, and then to the individual property holder. Locke felt that those who followed the law of nature, also understood as the law of reason, became the best because they held property. This narrowing will lead to the aggressive emphasis in social evolution as well as to the misunderstood use of Adam Smith as the champion of the greedy industrialist.

Opposing this narrowing trend was the development of the arcadian view of the place of humans within the ecosystem, a viewpoint developed as a counterthrust to the nearly overwhelming industrializing of society and human consciousness. The arcadian position, which developed additional strength in the nineteenth century, was begun, it appears, by a curate in Selborne named Gilbert White. His 1789 publication, *The Natural History of Selborne*, was a collection of his letters describing "the wildlife, seasons, and antiquities of his parish."[10] The theme that ran through these letters was White's awareness of the wholeness of the natural world[11] that included Selborne as microcosm: a single, interrelating entity that included humans.

This sense of oneness with nature stimulated Thoreau and underlay the Vitalism of the nineteenth century that developed as a theoretical antidote to mechanistic views of the developing scientific spirit, as well as an antidote to the Judeo-Christian tradition that saw external nature as the irresponsible servant of the male made in the image of God. Vitalism gave a mysterious power to nature that Aristotle would have found very unmysterious, a view that saw nature pulsating with the same spirit: a nature that was holistic and organic. Such thinking was also a counter to the positivism that evolved out of St. Simon's Golden Age theorizations.

But that positivism, heralded as a new age of science, proved to be too formidable an opponent for the arcadian movement, particularly after Darwin's *The Origin of Species by Means of Natural Selection* (1859, hereafter *Origin*) appeared to uncover the mysteries of historical life. But more than a century earlier, the Swede Linnaeus (Carl von Linne) had written his 1749 essay, "Oeconomia Naturae" (Economy of Nature), whose very title suggested that nature was something to be humanly managed. Although the essay had a holistic sense to it, Linnaeus wrote that everything may be made subservient to human use, and this included eliminating the ugly undesirables in nature and multiplying those aspects of nature useful or beautiful to humans.[12]

This denial of the human place *within*, and the affirmation of the human astride nature was given the status of "natural law" by the survival of the fittest clique that developed after Darwin's *Origin* and to some extent because of him. Even before Darwin, however, the arcadian movement seemed pushed, perhaps by their reaction to science, into a romantic view of nature that required an idealistic sense of human nature. And because the romantic, beneficent nature seemed countered by the violence and aggression evident on Galapagos Islands, it was simple to discard the idealism. In so doing, the truth of Hegel's ethical positions could be disregarded. For example, if the state were to be confused with civil society, and if its particular end is put down as the security and protection of property and personal freedom, then the interests of individuals as such become the ultimate goal of their association, and it follows that membership of the state is optional. But, Hegel argued, the state's relation to the individual is quite different from this. Since the state is mind objectified, it is *only* as one of its members that the individual himself has objectivity, genuine individuality, and an ethical life.[13]

The membership Hegel described, not very different from Cicero's perception, was a unity that overcame alienation between the subjective and the objective, but it was expressed far too idealistically for the nineteenth century. Marx, in adapting Hegel transformationally, materialized Hegel's concepts but did not, interestingly enough, improve on them, for it required as much idealistic faith to accept Hegel's alienation-overcoming unfolding of the *Weltgeist* as it did to believe with Marx that the socialization of the means of production would accomplish similar things.

Hence, these views could not stem the tide of a science that worshipped the concrete, the existential, and measurable phenomena. But with the emphasis on the discrete came discretion in its old meaning of discontinuity and disjunction. Unity and membership in that whole of nature, both human and nonhuman, was lost. And when survival of the fittest became a natural law describing the alleged human elevation over an external nature, the stage was set for Thomas Ewbank's 1855 *The World a Workshop*. Ewbank saw nature as existing only to serve human interests, and the world as the arena of human individualistic aggression and competition. This selfishness dominated both the external world and the internal nature of the human.[14] The world was a dangerous jungle, and, presumably, so was the internal human—a view that "original sinners" since the time of Augustine had always found palatable, for obvious reasons. Evolution was thought of as a weeding out process in which the weak or ill-adapted were gradually replaced by the adapted strong. So necessary was adaptation to this theory that notions of genetic mutation briefly appeared as explanation in J. Lamarck's *Philosophie Zoölogique* in 1809, the main thrust of which was that acquired characteristics are transmitted by the genes to the next generation. This revision of Mendelian inheritance enjoyed a brief heyday, but its defeat may have been more important than its success. The failure of Lamarck's explanation of environmentally induced genetic change seemed also to doom notions of hereditarial altruism and to underscore individual aggression rather than cooperation as the key to survival.

Kropotkin's ideas of mutualism mentioned in chapter 1 were partly shaped by his instinctive resistance to the dominant selfish ideas of his time but also by his anarchism. He needed to prove that people could and would help themselves if left alone and he needed internal drives to altruism to accomplish this goal. He saw this cooperation in the "jungle" of nineteenth-century Siberia and extrapolated it to humans, as had earlier been done by evolutionists to Darwin's research on animals. What is being genetically transmitted in Kropotkin's case, however, is cooperation, or altruism rather than aggression and selfishness.

Biologists who deal with genes resist these ideas and yet for centuries people have been taught that original sin, the disobedience of God in the Garden of Eden, was transmitted from generation to generation. Flying in the face of common sense, this belief imagined that a baby just two seconds old was already a sinner. How was sin transmitted if not through a genetic transfer of some kind? Similarly, aggression. Every action of that newly born baby could be interpreted as selfishness, as survival oriented. No doubt much of that explanation was correct. But all of it? The baby only takes, never gives? Nonsense. When these people talk about human nature they feel compelled to make it selfish, perhaps so they can argue that the unselfish, social human Karl Marx described as living in the new socialism was an impossibility.

So if we have for centuries believed in the genetic transmission of sin and selfishness why is there so much resistance to the idea of a genetic transference of cooperation and altruism? Genes are interesting things. There are, for example, cheating genes, or genes harmful to survival that find a place on the chromosome.[15]   Even more astounding is the work of Konrad Z. Lorenz, Nicholas Tinbergen, and Karl von Frisch reported by John Maynard Smith.[16] The work of these authors, wrote Smith, is a marriage of ethology and population genetics as demonstrated earlier by W. D. Hamilton. Parental altruism, for example, greatly increased the likelihood of genetic continuance of self-sacrificing behavior because it enhanced (even though it endangered) the survival of both the offspring and the parent.[17]

But those who describe altruistic behavior cannot leave it alone. They always seek to provide a selfish motivation for it, as though without the selfishness the behavior would not be real. For example, Smith described male baboons (male A and B) who were fighting over a female (C). Male A solicited the aid of Male D from the group passing by. After assisting A to win over B, D then left. Male A was thus victorious and presumably happy "forever after" with female C who, of course, was not asked her preference. Male B is simply out of luck, and Male D walks away. In order to have a selfish motive Smith introduces the notion of Robert Trivers, the idea of reciprocal altruism mentioned in Chapter 1. Smith wrote that the most convincing explanation of the evolution of this type of altruistic behavior between unrelated individuals was to be found in the concept of reciprocal altruism formulated by Trivers. According to Trivers' hypothesis, Smith felt, Male D by helping Male A (without increasing great personal risk), gains the assurance that on a future occasion Male A will help it in return. Hence Male D is most probably increasing its own Darwinian fitness, and the gene giving rise to this type of altruistic behavior will probably increase in frequency.[18]

Why do people strain so hard to find selfishness when altruism is so evident? Probably because they are uncomfortable at being described as altruists. For example, consider the story of John Peters (names are changed, but not the substantive content), a 911 dispatcher for a northern Michigan county. John earns $17,000 per year, has a wife and two children, one of whom has leukemia. In the spring of 1997 it was hoped that the little boy's leukemia was in remission, but by September it was obvious that it was not. John asked for unpaid leave so that he could transport his son to the University of Michigan Hospital in Ann Arbor and help his wife care for their son and daughter. When he called the chief deputy clerk to request his leave, she said to herself "This is ridiculous." She promptly wrote a memo to all 110 county employees and they donated their sick time to John so that he could continue to be paid. Altogether these fellow workers, who could have cashed out their surplus sick time, amassed 4½ months of sick time that the county officials agreed could be given to John and his family as salary. When the deputy county clerk was confronted with her unselfish activities, her response belittled the altruism, saying "We knew it could happen to us someday."[19]   The real reason for the altruism was John's need. The reason given, to play down the sacrifice, was reciprocity: "We only did it so that he could later do it for us." Ridiculous, but understandable. Few people can take a compliment gracefully. What one sees in this instance is a sophisticated rendering of "Aw shucks, ma'am, it weren't nothing." Fellow employees gave sick time, flowers, and toys to both the sick child and his sister. They sent lottery tickets, phone cards, gas cards, and food coupons to the young couple. A second infusion of sick time from other county employees gave seventy-six more days so that John could stay with his sick son into the summer without losing salary. That additional time unfortunately was not needed. The child died in late April holding both of his parent's hands. That gift to the child and to his parents flowed out of the loving in the hearts of county employees.[20]

Other behaviors besides altruism are transmitted genetically. Fear is evidently also genetically transmitted. James Miller, in his *Living Systems*, cited the example of monkeys reared in isolation, receiving visual imputs only from colored slides of other monkeys in various activities and of other scenes that contained no monkeys at all. Between 2½ and 4 months of age, he wrote, the monkey subjects reacted strongly to pictures of monkeys in threatening postures, and rarely touched a lever that turned on such pictures. These apparently inborn fear reactions seemed to be responses to signals between monkeys that are innately decodable.[21]

This is analogous to Hebb's discussion of the human infant's fear of strangers, which depends on the recognition of loved ones, that in turn sounds similar to Lorenz' description of imprinting. Hebb argued that the behavior of infants in expressing a fear of strangers is learned behavior that depends on a maturation of the nervous system. However, Hebb argued that the dichotomy between learned and instinctive behavior is in many cases false. A false opposition of the "instinctive" to the "learned," he wrote, has tended in the past to prevent us from seeing these common features of human behavior and from recognizing that they must result, much as the instinctive behavior of rodent and carnivore does from the way we are made, and the universal features of the human environment.[22]

The point made here by Miller about young monkeys is that even though this behavior can in some senses be called learned, it does have a genetic foundation. He wrote that several studies on the development of the nervous system have tipped the balance toward the relatively greater importance of inherited neural organization and assign relatively less importance to learning. Sperry maintains, Miller wrote, that the genetically determined aspects of neural processes even in so-called "learned" behavior, may be much more complex than those aspects superimposed by experiential information inputs.[23]

The transmission of fear reactions in monkeys by heredity is analogous to the concept of genetic evolution of altruism. Our problem appears to be that we have lacked the mental ability to say so. We seem able in our long his/herstory to recognize the symbiosis between human and nature, but the language used to articulate the unity is so culturally or historically conditioned that it appears far more different than it is. Cicero described the similitude between God and human, and in another place referred to natural law as the mind of God. Augustine used similar words, and meant much the same thing. Aquinas wrote about God imprinting principles of proper actions on humans. The problem of his age and a legacy of Christianity caused him to see this as coming from outside rather than from within the person. Aquinas' impression of an inward active principle is Aristotle's form or inward principle of growth which also arose from within the individual.

Immanuel Kant put this in language that was advanced for his day when he wrote that the sense of moral consciousness does not come from experience but is a part of our inherent psychological structure, like his categories of perception were—and that that sense of moral consciousness is an internal tribunal present in every person in every race, and is absolute, commanding us unconditionally and without exception or excuse to do what is right for its own sake as an end in itself, not as a means to happiness or reward or some other good. Its imperative is categorical, taking two forms: Act in such a way that if all others acted similarly everything would be well, and act in such a way that you treat each as an end and not as a means.[24] This is an objectification of the subjective along the lines Hegel followed when he wrote that unification pure and simple was the true content and aim of the individual, and the individual's destiny was the living of a universal life.

In an article published late in his life, when the fear of censors and the need for staying employed was less pressing, Kant wrote that God was not a substance existing outside the human, but was rather a creation of human reason, prefiguring Ludwig Feuerbach's statement that people created God rather than the other way around. Kant wrote "God is *not a substance existing outside me*, but merely a moral relation within me. The categorical imperative does not assume a substance issuing its commands from on high, conceived therefore as outside me, but is a commandment or a prohibition of my own reason".[25]

The categorical imperative, in other words, represented to Kant human duties as divine commandments—not in the historical sense, as if a divine being had actually given commands to a person, but in the sense that human reason has power to command with the authority and in the guise of a deity. The *idea* of such a being arises out of the categorical imperative, and not vice-versa. The Supreme Being is a creation of reason not an external substance.[26]

Ernst Troelst seemed to be saying much the same thing when he wrote about natural law at the end of World War I. He spoke of the ideal as emanating from what he called "an indestructable moral core." [27] Gierke seemed to be paraphrasing Kant when he wrote that if there is to be an obligatory external standard for the action of will in general, and not merely for the action of this or that particular will, such a standard must be rooted and grounded in a spiritual force that confronts the will as something independent. That force is Reason.[28]

There is a great deal of philosophy lying there to be picked up, but suffice it to say that altruism appears to be a voice of reason operating within us that has evolved with us over time. Part of the problem of recognizing the vitality of that altruism might be the problem of expression. David Ritchie, another philosopher of natural law, described the problem as assuming a fullness deep in the past that might better be expressed as an evolutionary growth from small to larger. The defect of the theory, he wrote, lay in the tendency to set this ideal in abstract antithesis against the actual and the historical. In light of the conception of evolution applied to human society (i.e., using an historical method in the study of institutions, and being influenced by an historical spirit in dealing with all human problems) we must think of this Divine purpose as something gradually revealing itself in the education of the human race.

> In other words, an adequate theory of rights and an adequate theory of the State must rest upon a philosophy of history; and steady progress in political and social reform cannot be made unless there is a willingness to learn the lessons of experience, and a reasonable reverence for the long toil of the human spirit in that past from which we inherit not only our problems, but the hope and the means of their solution.[29]

Has altruism evolved with the rest of life, developed as a part of the human nature we say we possess? An affirmative answer seems imperative, and yet such an answer demands an awareness as well, that such an evolved altruism makes it the unwritten law of human nature. Jacques Maritain wrote in 1943 that:

> This means that there is, by very virtue of human nature *an order or a disposition which human reason can discover and according to which the human will must act in order to attune itself to the necessary ends of the human being. The unwritten law, or natural law, is nothing more than that.*[30]

And this means nothing less than that altruism is natural, as natural as the aggression we are so quick to imagine as the whole of our nature.

Konrad Lorenz, in arguing that aggression is natural and indeed useful to species evolution, never meant to justify or vindicate aggression. Quite the contrary, according to Donald Campbell. Yet it unfortunately remains true in the present climate, he said, that labeling aggression as "natural" may well have the effect of labeling it "normal" and "good." Perhaps we should educate ourselves away from this overly simplified morality, he wrote, back toward that distrust of human nature found in our religious traditions.[31] That, however, would take us the wrong way. The distrust of human nature and the reemphasis of original sin is only necessary because we have forgotten the balance in our evolution: altruism along with the aggression. Both are a natural part of us. Only when one subtracts natural altruism from the human character does our nature seem our biggest problem. But when we see the balance, we will see ourselves correctly for the first time in our history.

And it is time for that recognition. As population grows, and food, water and energy shortages converge, the need to plan for a positive human future is increasingly clear. Failure to develop such plans because we see ourselves as selfish aggressors barely held in check by government and church can doom our endangered species to the depressing finale depicted most elegantly in Jean Raspail's *Camp of the Saints*. And if Victor Ferkiss is correct in assuming that the evolved (or created) human is the moral consciousness of the whole of nature, our responsibilities are indeed great.[32] Coming to understand this balance of altruism and selfishness does not involve us in grafting something new onto the human character, like a Sunday suit on a dirty body, but a recognition of what was there all along.

NOTES

1. Cicero, *On the Commonwealth*, Book III, chap. 11, 22, cited in Brendan Brown, *The Natural Law Reader* (New York: Oceana Publications, 1960), pp. 54–55.

2. Ludwig Feuerbach, "Preliminary Theses for a Reform of Philosophy," *Anecdota*, February 1843.

3. Cicero, *On the Commonwealth*.

4. Ibid., pp. 57–58.

5. Milton Mayerhoff, *On Caring* (New York: Harper & Row, 1971), p. 30.

6. Ibid., p. 48.

7. St. Thomas Aquinas, trans. Fathers of the English Dominican Province, *Summa Theologica* (New York: Benziger Bros., 1947), I, p. 1-11, Art. 2: p. 996; cited in Brian R. Nelson, *Western Political Thought from Socrates to the Age of Ideology*, Second Edition (Englewood Cliffs, New

Jersey: Prentice-Hall, 1996), p. 127.

    8. John Locke, *Second Treatise*, chap. ll, sec. 135, in Ernest Barker, ed., *Social Contract* (London: Oxford University Press, 1947), p. 114.

    9. William Bluhm, *Theories of the Political System*, Second Edition (Englewood Cliffs, NJ: Prentice Hall, Inc., 1971), p. 349.

    10. Donald Worster, *Nature's Economy* (San Francisco: Sierra Club Books, 1977), p. 5.

    11. See Chapter Nine where this topic is grappled with in some detail.

    12. Linnaeus, "Oeconomia Naturae" in Vol 2 of Johann C. D. Screber, ed., *Amoenitates academicae seu dissertationes variae physicae, medicae, botanicae antehac seorsim editae nunc collectae et auctae cum tabulis, aeneis* (Erlangen, J. J. Palm, 1785-1790).

    13. G. Hegel, *Philosophy of Right*, T. M. Knox, trans. (London: Oxford University Press, 1942), p. 156.

    14. Thomas Ewbank, *The World A Workshop, or, The Physical Relation of Man to the Earth* (New York, D. Appleton Co., 1855).

    15. James F. Crow, "Genes that Violate Mendel's Rules," *Scientific American*, 240, 2, (February 1979), pp. 134ff.

    16. John Maynard Smith, "Evolution of Behavior," *Scientific American*, 239, 3 (September 1978), pp. 176ff.

    17. Ibid., p. 178.

    18. Ibid., p. 184.

    19. Susan Ager, "West Branch Man Gets A Gift of Time," *Detroit Free Press*, October 12, 1997, p. F1.

    20. Ibid., "Open hearts build path back to work," May 3, 1998, p. J1.

    21. James Miller, *Living Systems* (New York: McGraw-Hill, 1978), p. 471.

    22. Donald Olding Hebb, *A Textbook of Psychology* (Philadelphia: W. B. Saunders, 1958), p. 126.

    23. Miller, *Living Systems*, p. 471, citing R. W. Sperry, "Developmental Basis of Behavior," in A. Roe and G. G. Simpson, eds., *Behavior and Evolution* (New Haven, CT: Yale University Press, 1958), pp. 128–139.

    24. Immanuel Kant, *The Critique of Pure Reason, The Critique of Practical Reason and other Ethical Treaties, and the Critique of Judgment* published by the University of Chicago in the Great Books tradition. The categorical imperative is found especially in *The Critique of Practical Reason*, p. 302, for example. Kant is difficult to read, however. He was trying to outfox his censor and made things unnecessarily difficult.

    25. Immanuel Kant, *Opus postumum*, cited in Will and Auriel Durant, *Rousseau and Revolution* (New York: Simon & Schuster, 1967), vol X of *The Story of Civilization*, p. 550.

26. Ibid.

27. Ernst Troelst, in Otto Gierke, *Natural Law and the Theory of Society 1500–1800* (Boston: Beacon Press, 1957), p. 218.

28. Otto Gierke, *Natural Law and the Theory of Society 1500-1800* (Boston. Beacon Press, 1957), pp. 224–225.

29. David Ritchie, *Natural Rights* (London: George Allen & Unwin, 1894), p. 286.

30. Jacques Maritain, *The Rights of Man and Natural Law*, Doris C. Anson, trans. (New York: Charles Scribner's Sons, 1943), p. 61.

31. Donald Campbell, "Reintroducing Konrad Lorenz to Psychology," in Richard Evans, *Konrad Lorenz: The Man and His Ideas* (New York: Harcourt Brace Jovanovich, 1975), p. 99.

32. Victor Ferkiss, *The Future of Technological Civilization* (New York: Brazillier, 1974).

Chapter 3

Altruism as Social Instinct

Sociability is one of the characteristics normally associated with being human. Dining together, for example, has been cited as a particularly human activity.[1] Socialness is a very early determiner of who and what was human, and sociability is simply another word for altruism. This can be seen the moment a discussion of altruism takes place. The discussants are immediately plunged into a description of human behavior with others and with the world around them -- animals, plants, air, dirt, and stones. Altruism cannot help but be social behavior involving togetherness, relationships, bonding, connectedness, and community. Sometimes the behavior is between individuals, whereas at other times social groups are involved, where individual or group actions affect a larger whole. What is not being described is altruism's opposite: selfishness, the language of alienation, of individualism, of divorce, of competition and capitalism. Altruism lends itself to would-be saints while the greeds and lusts of selfishness create stereotypes of evil, disgrace, and ruin.

One of the dimensions of altruism, then, so obvious that it is sometimes overlooked, is that it is an instinct for group survival, supporting a continuance of existence in instances where selfish behavior that might seem the obvious choice would yield opposite results. Altruism in this instance means activity by individuals that benefits the group at some individual risk.

Such behavior in human relationships has been the object of concern for centuries, since people have had the ability and time to contemplate, analyze, and write. This concern, usually ethical, was expressed as a description of how people relate, or how they ought to relate. Sometimes this moral awareness would focus on individual behavior in relation to a deity, spirit, or light, or would encompass a social ethic wherein the societal unit was conceived as a collective person. In the ancient world, both individual and social ethicists sought self-sufficiency; the Cynics and Stoics sought it by withdrawal from society, whereas Plato and Aristotle sought it as a collective possibility. Membership was a core component of the definition of human. Aristotle, for example, argued that to be a human meant being a member of a larger whole. Self-sufficiency was, as it was with Plato, social, not individual. Outside a political society, Aristotle argued, a person was either a beast or a god. Definitely not a human. Self-sufficiency was achieved, it seemed, either by withdrawing from society or by membership in that society.

In interesting ways, this dichotomy continues in modern times; the same goal sought by very different means. Withdrawal or membership is used as a template to judge ourselves and others. Think, for a moment, of the debate we used to have between hard and soft technology as the way in which the United States (and the rest of the world) should progress in the future. The hard technologists stressed capital-intensive economies, powered by electricity from centralized generating stations, often nuclear. The soft technologists, on the other hand, stressed a more labor-intensive economic approach, relying heavily on decentralized sources of energy such as windmills and solar power. Very often there was an underlying ethical philosophy for each side, and this is what was really interesting. The hard technology people articulated an ethic of competition and separation whereas the soft technologists talked about cooperation and compassion. The lines of selfishness and altruism were not clearly drawn, but they were always present; even if at times the lines were difficult to draw. For example, a decentralized approach might have been more competitive than a centralized monopoly seeking to restrict competition, but it is also true that a cooperative, decentralized approach could be overorganized and could function just like a monopoly.

This argument is sometimes articulated in terms of progress versus environmental concerns with the "progress people" joining the struggle as allies of the hard technologists. In chapter 8, the notion of progress is discussed in the context of misplaced altruism; but for now suffice it to state that progress people are often stereotyped as individual entrepreneurs who see profit as their only goal. The private good—profit—completely overshadows, perhaps even obliterates social goods like clean air or water. Environmentalists are stereotyped as mindless advocates of zero economic growth, opponents of nuclear power and hydroelectric facilities and as people with no alternatives for energy production, more concerned with endangered species than with jobs for humans. When one cuts through the ideological overgrowth there seems to be the same debate: It is either the nature of the human to compete, aggress, dominate, and be an individual, or, contrariwise, to cooperate, seek peace, and to sense oneself as part of a larger and significant whole. Little recognition is ever given to the possibility that both these forces can be present in the same individual or that people will have these positions in varying degrees of intensity. When one side preaches to the other, therefore, it is usually the absolutely correct telling the absolutely incorrect of their errors.

Underlying all these words is that simple template of altruism versus selfishness. This may appear reductionistic, but the longer the subject is studied the more apparent is the dichotomy and the labels on its ends. The people who advocate one side or the other make absolute enemies of the other side, despised as an evil. Serious opposition, for example, to nuclear fission as a source of electricity was also taken as a blast against competition, capitalism, and the American way of life. The argumentative leaps make no sense, but the logic appears understandable. An advocate of a new shopping mall also wants to deprive the poor of food stamps? Deny poor women prenatal care? People think reductionistically. Liberals intent on extending welfare or feeding the world like Edward O. Wilson[2] are confronted by advocates of selfishness, such as Garrett Hardin[3] and Hardin and Baden.[4] The selfish side sounds a bit like Social Darwinists at the turn of the century who preferred to let nature care for the drunks in the gutter, rather than help them up so that they can go home. The liberals, on the other hand, sound like they agree with a brochure from Focus Hope, which seems to sum up the altruistic side. "[G]ive now so that through HOPE you may continue to embrace our one humanity."[5]

This discussion, however, is very old. Aristotle was a biologist who argued that people were social or community oriented by nature. In other words, our instincts seek our survival but they also seek socialness or social survival rather than the preservation of the individual. Humans, Aristotle and Aquinas argued, are social by nature, or naturally social. Humans were not a loose collection of hostile individualists to whom the community was an artificial creation, an idealized republic such as Plato, had imagined, but an entirely natural phenomenon which grew out of the nature of the human. If he were writing today, Aristotle might speak of the impulse to community emerging from the limbic system of the brain, or about the possibility of a gene for community-oriented behavior. Aristotle felt so strongly about the naturalness of the community that he argued in his *Politics* that the state was logically prior to the individual. Outside the political system, he argued, a person was definitely not a human. The socialness was an intrinsic part of the definition of humanness. It was not an add-on, nor something artificial and external to the human, but internal, as though it was indeed carried by the genes.

This meant that virtue was relational to Aristotle. He could not conceive of virtue in isolation. Altruism in human and animal behavior was social as well as survival in nature. In *Ethics*, Aristotle made sure the reader understood, in the midst of all the conditional syllogisms, that virtue was the means to the end of happiness, but that happiness could not be achieved outside of a social whole—indeed it was unimaginable. It was only in a polis, or political system, that people could be virtuous, and, therefore, happy. So, Aristotle argued, lodged already in the definition of the human is the instinct toward socialness.

This also was how the ancient Stoics saw it. Ethical social obligations that we have toward one another exist by nature and are universally valid. As discussed in chapter 2, these obligations could be called natural law—laws of moral reason embedded in a person's consciousness and reflecting the larger rational ethical order of the universe. Cicero, an eclectic Roman thinker, argued in vain for the old Roman Commonwealth rather than the new Roman Empire, and defined the desired commonwealth as "the people's affair; and the people is not every group of [humans], associated in any manner, but is the coming together of a considerable number of [people] who are united by a common agreement about law and rights and by the desire to participate in mutual advantages."[6]

Moreover, he thought, the original cause of this coming together is a kind of natural social instinct.[7] This instinct seems also to have been the basis of the *humanitas* articulated by the rather heavily Stoic Scipionic Circle in Rome. This concept, similar to the Scots "mense," refers to goodness, decency, civility, and grace.

Edward Wilson wrote:

> The question of interest is no longer whether human social behavior is genetically determined; .it is to what extent. The accumulated evidence for a large hereditary component is more detailed and compelling than most persons, even geneticists, realize. I will go further; it already is decisive.[8]

Wilson was writing of social behavior in general. Altruism–selfishness behavior is one aspect of that socialness, and the observation of similar behavior in the nonhuman world strengthens the argument that genes are involved—genes possessed by both humans and animals. This is a very complicated story. If the full human genome from one person were ever printed out on paper, it would take up to two hundred volumes the size of a telephone book, each containing 1,000 pages each, or 200,000 phone directory-sized pages.[9] Humans and most animals are amazingly complex.

Behavior driven by genes not only pushes in the direction of virtue, but also in the direction of social connectedness, as though the connectedness and the virtue were the same thing. Think of the potentially sacrificial nature of the horses Peter Kropotkin watched in Siberia who formed a ring to ward off the attacking wolves. Who was being benefited by the ringed horses? Not one in particular or even a clique, but the entire group. The horses must see their own individual survival as needing the whole. The animal or human in question is instinctually groping for social survival.

Look at another example. An alarmed Red-necked Pademelon, a variety of Australian wallaby, will give two or more thumps of the rear foot when threatened, alerting others to the danger.[10] This seems to be an instinctual kindness, an example of social or community caring, a social altruism that bends the survival of the fittest to a collective rather than to the individual. Even African wild dogs possess a community sense.

These animal studies seem strikingly analogous to the work done by that subset of biology and zoology called *sociobiology*. The term, which enjoyed a brief popularity, was also part of the title of Wilson's book, *Sociobiology: The New Synthesis*. This research redirected one's attention not only to cooperative behavior among animals, but also to the sort of activity that intrigued Kropotkin (i.e., social activity that could be called mutual aid). It could also be called *social altruism* because the animal examples still refer to self-sacrificing behavior that benefits another individual or group. Think back to the ring of horses collectively fighting the wolves. If genetic instincts were only for individual survival, the horses behaved strangely. Perhaps some horses would be dumb enough to stay in that ring, but surely others would escape the endangered collective, and evolution would select for the escapees because of their greater chance of survival. But this does not appear to be the case among animals or humans. Think of a battlefield situation where an individual soldier may throw himself on the grenade so as to save the rest of the group. This is the sort of instinctual altruism that is more common among animals than one might think.

In addition, the findings of sociobiology help repudiate the one-sided competitive or aggressive interpretation of Darwin. How could behavior that reduces an individual chance for survival have evolved in a natural selection that favored only traits that improved individual survival? If nature and the nature of humans were so selfish, the whole world by now should have become a Hobbesian war of all against all. Any animals or humans exhibiting altruistic behavior should have died out, while their more selfish comrades prospered. But this has not been the case. Even among animals that may seem to be selfish individualists, evolution has a built-in capacity for cooperation and sacrifice when the living conditions warrant it.

With genetic evolution in mind, sociobiologists search for ways in which the myriad forms of social organization adapt a particular species to the specific opportunities and dangers encountered in their environment. Although one might not think of awarding a medal to a robin or a thrush, these birds frequently endanger themselves when they issue a warning to others of approaching danger. The thin reedy whistle of the titmouse is another example. Why draw attention to oneself, why not just fly away? Paul W. Sherman called this activity nepotism rather than social altruism because it seemed motivated by the preservation of kin, particularly the family line or what Hardin called the germ line.[11] But was this because the squirrel warned kin or because kin were the only ones around to hear the warning? Sherman's new term may simply describe an accidental massing of kin. He may not have wanted to call these warnings altruism but they certainly were. Exceptions to this more narrow motivation do seem to exist, however. Hence the term *altruism* may have a more generalized accuracy when one moves beyond the Belding's ground squirrels that Sherman studied.

Whales that periodically beach themselves may be motivated by the difficulties of one of their number. This has been one of the major interpretations of that activity. Dolphins will gather around a wounded member and raise it to the surface so as to allow the animal to breathe. African wild dogs go off on a hunt and then, returning, regurgitate food so that pups and adults left behind to guard the pups can also eat. And, interestingly, even crippled and sick old dogs who could not do much guarding shared in the food and survived longer because of the cooperative generosity of the hunting dogs. The social behavior of monk parakeets also supports the notion of a social altruism. Breeding pairs are often assisted by a third monk parakeet who does important things like helping to build the nest or bringing the female food. This helper may be a relative, but not necessarily. The point is the social altruism.[12] The fittest who survive seem to be serendipitously helped to survive by a "stranger" in the group.

Adult chimps in Tanzania who adopt young orphans were adopting their closest relatives. Although this fact makes the adoption sound less altruistic, perhaps related young chimps were all they knew because unrelated young chimps lived too far away. And what about the ant soldier on the losing side of the ant war who is adopted rather than killed by the other side? Kin survival is important but it apparently is not the only motivation. Group activity by bees wherein honey bees commit suicide to protect the queen and others look like kin survival, or group solidarity focused on kin protection. On the other hand, burying beetles (nicrophorus) often work in mated pairs to bury a dead mouse in which they have laid their eggs. Many times other beetles will work alongside the mated pair, helping to dig the hole and to bury the mouse. Then they will simply depart. That sounds like altruism of a much broader sort than merely survival of the germ line—more like survival of the species.[13]

Sociobiologists believe that the capacity to sacrifice for the group is a part of genetic evolution rather than environmentally learned behavior. This has unfortunately led some to read into their work a more generalized genetic determinism that could underlie theories of genetic racial inferiority.[14] This is unfortunate, for what the sociobiologist was saying is that natural selection is broad enough to include kin or group selection. The self-sacrificing honey bee or termite soldier protects the colony collective, leaving the protected ones to flourish, brothers and sisters of the fallen, and they are the ones who continue the multiplication of the altruistic genes.

Some people do not want to consider these acts altruistic because they doubt the existence of altruism. Such commentators insist on portraying such apparently altruistic behavior in terms of selfishness, even that which appears to be decidedly altruistic, such as a soldier throwing himself on a live grenade to save the group. This rush to explain away altruism an be summed up in three forms. First, the action that appears altruistic is said to benefit only the kin of the do-gooder. Thus, in a biologically forward sense the altruistic act is actually selfish because one is preserving one's own gene line. Second, the altruism is only apparent, almost as though altruism was impossible. The real motivation, it is said, is fear, and the signal is not so much to warn others as it is designed to protect the warner through group activity. The kindness is actually a very clever selfishness. Third, the apparent altruism occurs in an ambience of reciprocity; the supposed altruistic behavior is done to others so that at a later time altruistic behavior will be done to me. Again a selfish motive.

As an illustration of the first sort of explaining away of altruism think of the Belding ground squirrels studied by Sherman.[15] He felt that it was only the kin that were warned. Because the individual squirrel's own genetic line was being protected by the warning, Sherman called the behavior nepotism rather than altruism, suggesting that altruism could only be said to exist when the benefiting recipient was not related. The importance of the recipient relationship seemed to be a spin-off of Hardin's concern to justify selfishness that protects one's own germ line. Sherman's use of the kin argument does the same thing by denying the altruism.

There is no question that protection of one's own genetic line is an important survival strategy, but in order to demonstrate Sherman's point properly, a control group would be necessary. For example, if the squirrel kins were mixed up, would the alarm signals not be given? Or would the alarm signals come in some sort of kin-code so that only ones own genetic line would benefit? If this were demonstrated, Sherman's explaining away of altruism would be acceptable. But in the context of the Belding ground squirrels, the alarm signals were given to everyone and if only the kin could hear the signal it was because only they were close enough to hear the alarm. An alternative explanation is that the motivation for the signal is not primarily the protection of kin, but the need to protect the other squirrels, even if kin are the only ones to benefit.

An example of the second attempt to explain away altruism (the altruism is only apparent) is the book by Richard Dawkins, *The Selfish Gene*.[16] Dawkins felt that a selfish explanation for alarm calls was warranted because of the danger attached to the giving of the signal. His examples, however, are anthropomorphisms. For example, he argued that the warner may be aware that if he or she did not warn, the less sharp-eyed members of the group, who did not notice the approaching predator, would be spotted anyway. The potential warner, in other words, would be endangered with the rest—hence the warning. What appears to be altruism is in fact motivated by the individual's selfish desire to stay alive. The warner is primarily protecting itself, it is said, and only secondarily, almost accidentally, the group.

Dawkins confused gene with gene machine or body and results with motivation. The thesis of his interesting book is that genes always act selfishly. There is no quarrel with this position if one is discussing gene interactions with each other to achieve a position on the chromosome. Although selfishness here makes survival sense for the gene it does not indicate a successful strategy for the gene machine. Keep in mind that what is being discussed here is not group selection, but an individual, preprogrammed instinct for action of one sort or another that over time has benefitted the individual as well as the group. And, even though the results of the warning may be kin survival or even self-survival, the motivation was to warn—to alert the group to danger at the risk of exposing oneself. That's altruism. If it quacks like a duck, and so on.

A stable evolutionary strategy, it is suggested, is to act selfishly sometimes, perhaps even most of the time, but at other times to act altruistically when the instinct guides in that direction. And when the latter occurs, it is not the appearance of altruism but the real thing. Despite the obvious nature of the argument, attempts to deny the altruism continue to be made. Tim Clutton-Brock and his colleagues at Cambridge University published an article in *Science* in which they seek to demonstrate that meerkats, an African mongoose that looks like a bit like a prairie dog or a squirrel, are not altruistic as previously imagined, but quite selfish. The report on the article in *The Economist* described the notion of animal altruism as an anthromorphic fable. The fact that meerkats were guarded by one of their kind was described as not altruistic because there was no risk that the study observed. So no meerkat sacrificed to save the group. Shall we call this potential altruism? And what about the meerkat collaboration to raise the young, such as the non-breeding females and males not the father who bring food to the pups, or babysit the pups? Why is there such a push to deny the obvious and sneer at those who call it the way it appears to be?[17] Scientists observe, report on what they observe, and theorize about what they have observed. All this is well and good. But theories can be empirically based or essentially based. The former creates a theory that explains the observed, drawn from the heart of and the ambience of the observed. The latter provides theories that come from assumptions and beliefs that were held prior to the observations. The belief that all animals are selfish, for example. This is not science, it is bad rationalizing, like most theology.

The third way of explaining away altruism is associated with the name of Trivers. This is the notion of reciprocal altruism. Even though the activity is done for someone else at some cost to oneself, the activity is not called altruism but selfishness because of the expectation the giver has of being the recipient in the future. A does a kindness for B so that a kindness will later be done for A. This has a surface plausibility because there are so many situations where such reciprocity is expected. Politicians will vote for a bill they do not like in order to gain a later vote from a colleague on another bill that the colleague does not like. But reciprocal relationships are tricky—they require monitoring for effectiveness. Two friends, for example, interacting with each other, will quickly notice when the reciprocity becomes onesided.

Think of the possibility that Party A is driving down the expressway and sees Party B in trouble on the side of the road. The situation is classic in the sense that the need is very visible, the traffic is light enough so that stopping to help will not endanger Party A or others in addition to Party B, and it is early enough in the day so that a fear of strange areas at night has not been activated. Moreover, Party A's has no compelling reason not to stop (i.e., he has no pressing appointments, no pregnant wife whose water has just broke; just the desire to get to the destination in a reasonable time). Will Party A stop to help Party B? Trivers would argue that if assistance were provided by Party A, it would be done so that Party B could later offer him assistance. The benefit of the original helper drives the bus here. But no evidence is ever provided to support this idea. The reciprocity is assumed so that no one will possibly imagine Party A as altruistic. Why? Because altruism does not fit the harsh world of the fit surviving. Reciprocity is read onto a situation so as to change the altruism into a selfishness that matches the preconception of the observer. There is also no reason to assume that if a person helped another who was in some sort of traffic accident, that the helper's motivation was to later receive assistance from that person. When reciprocity is broadened to the group level, and there is no monitoring, one has a forced conceptualization of an environmentally stable strategy rather than an explanation for altruism. In the highway example, the request for assistance was triggered by Party B's need. The assistance was triggered by the need in another.

Think of the example of Shannon Wright, a sixth-grade English teacher in Jonesboro, Arkansas. On a Tuesday afternoon, March 24, 1998, shooters fired weapons at school children. Mrs. Wright, 32, put her body between the gun and a young girl named Emma at whom the rifle was aimed. Mrs. Wright died that evening. A sixth-grader who saw the whole thing said: "This guy was aiming at Emma. He was fixing to shoot her and Mrs. Wright moved in front of her. She got shot. She did. I watched her."[18] What is the behavior one is witnessing? Altruism. To use the notion of reciprocity to deny the altruism means that there is some bank account up in the sky where people's kindnesses are both stored and monitored for later use. This kind of thinking seems silly and it obscures and invalidates the very real worth of the altruistic action.

Robert A. Daniels studied a species of small, bottom-dwelling fish called *harpagifer bispinis* in the coves of the Anarctic Peninsula.[19] In a series of dives, as well as in laboratory tests, Daniels watched females prepare nest sites and spawn in the summer. If the female were not disturbed, she might guard the eggs for four to five months until they hatched. If the mother were removed by natural or human intervention, another fish, usually male, would take over the guarding, and if it were also removed, a third fish would assume the guard duties. Kinship was not always involved because unrelated fish would take the guard role as frequently as kin. There was a danger from predators (seals), and there could be no individual benefit then or later. Reciprocity could not be involved, Daniels felt, because the replacement guard fish was permanently removed from the group and could not later reciprocate the kindness. What is the reason? Altruism, triggered by the need just as in Glenn Zorpette's monk parakeet example.[20]

If altruism and selfishness are both possible responses to the need in another, and if the response is sometimes altruism and sometimes selfishness, could there not be a ratio of altruism to selfishness in animal and human behavior? In the baboon study done by Craig Packer in Tanzania, referred to in chapter 2, Packer reported one hundred forty instances of male baboon solicitation of help in some kind of contest. Twenty of these instances were situations where two males fought over an estrous female. A third male, asked to help one of the fighters, had the option of aiding or walking on by.[21] Fourteen out of the twenty cases, the third male acted selfishly and walked on by. Six times the third male stayed to help. If this were a game the score would read Altruism 6, Selfishness 14. The baboons in the observation, who had the option of going either way, chose to act altruistically 30 percent of the time and selfishly 70 percent.

No one wants to build a mountain on a match-stick by assuming that all male baboons always operate on this 30/70 ratio or that it illustrates human behavior. What can be welcomed, however, is the notion that the idea of a ratio between altruism and selfishness gets us away from absolutes, from only saints and only sinners, to the real world in which people sometimes act altruistically and sometimes not. This idea has for years made intuitive sense to my students who have discovered in themselves ratios ranging from 40/60 to 10/90. Humans do act as though such a ratio exists, as though attempts to operationalize their response to need would reveal a fairly consistent ratio even if it were not the 30/70 of the baboon study. Indeed weighting the ratio toward selfishness seems to describe human behavior quite well without making it absolutely or totally selfish.

If such a ratio can be assumed, this is further suggestive evidence that the genes carry both behaviors as potential responses to need in others. This possibility might be described as a behavioral allele, a genetic proclivity to respond in one way or another when confronted by the appropriate stimulus. This way of considering the matter uses the word *allele* in a different sense than that normally used in genetics. Instead of the word describing rival genes, it is here used to describe rival behaviors carried by a single gene. Physical genes for eye color, for example, are distinguished from behavioral genes that probably cannot code specific behaviors in advance. Otherwise the human or animal would be too limited. Just as for many another organization, preprogrammed, rigid behavior is not survival oriented.

Although this may be true, it should not be taken to mean that externals have no influence on genetic development or the relation between genes and behavior. Note that what is being referenced here is the relation between external, epiphenomenal stimuli and the genes, not the relation between externals and behavior that ignores the genetic element. Behaviorist psychology, for example, is not under attack here, it is simply not being discussed. Instead, the reference is to the influence external stimuli may have on the genetic component of the human, with the possibility of altering not simply an individual's behavior, but the very nature of the human. Two examples may suffice to illustrate the discussion.

First, the words of Stuart A. Altmann, a biologist at the University of Chicago who spoke at the University of Michigan in March 1979. The behavioral ecology of animals, he said, becomes progressively less relevant to human behavior as human welfare becomes independent of local ecology. My own welfare, survival, and reproductive success, he said, are buffered from my local environment by a complex cultural system involving housing, clothing, long-range transport of food, fuel, and so on, so that extreme fluctuations in my ambient temperature, availability of food, water, and other resources are eliminated. Not surprisingly, my behavior and social relationships are largely independent of environmental conditions in my local home town.[22]

Humans are buffered from their environments in a number of ways. The prehistoric food sharing behavior of hominids that appears to have begun the distinction between human and nonhuman lines of development, supplemented by the tremendous cultural evolutionary explosion, has buffered humans from interacting directly with their environment. This environmental alienation is what is frequently considered progress. Not only does this suggest, as Altmann argued, that this buffering makes the behavior of baboons and humans less comparable, but it also implies that in large cities, where humans are not only disconnected from their environment in the usual sense, but are also buffered or alienated from each other, that the altruism–selfishness ratio is likely to veer toward the selfish side. In a large city such as New York or Chicago, the ratio may well be 10/90 rather than the earlier assumption of the possibility of 30/70.

Because acquired characteristics are not passed by genes, the nature of our altruistic–selfish ratio is perhaps shaped by cultural nurturing. Frequent, if not constant, barrages of "don't get involved" or "don't help—it's none of our business" or "it's safer to be selfish" in one variety or another from urban parents and peers could sway the actual ratio from say a 30/70 to the 10/90. This may not be the entire explanation.

Work on brain chemistry argues that the brain has three fundamental signalling processes. First, direct transmission of signals from nerve cell to nerve cell. Second, the modulation of the message analogous to changing the volume of a radio. Third, the sending of chemicals to the body affecting all the cells equipped to handle the hormonal message—analogous to a radio broadcast. Urban life, it is conjectured, may create a chemical environment inside the body that prompts more individual selfishness and less social altruism. Earlier experiments that showed a high correlation between crowding and aggression in laboratory animals bear this out as well as occasional news reports from cities indicating a gross sort of selfishness wherein aware people turn away *en masse* from the obvious need of another and even jeer rather than aid an unfortunate individual in a life-threatening situation.

The second example of the importance of externals can be called the nature of the environmental challenge. Richard Lewontin argued in *The Scientific American*[23] that adaptation is the process of evolutionary change whereby the organism provides a better and better "solution" to the "problem" thrown up by experience. Bertrand Russell observed another facet of this situation. "If evolutionary ethics were sound, we ought to be entirely indifferent as to what the course of evolution might be, since whatever it is, it is thereby proved to be the best."[24] The better solution mentioned by Lewontin may imply to some a purposiveness to evolution that Russell refuted. The process of adaptation, which is actually another way of saying evolution, may cause a development of human nature that one is not indifferent to; not because one reads onto evolutionary history a purposiveness that is not there, but because one is aware of being in evolution rather than being the result of evolution. When Russell used the word "best" he meant best for survival, but some forms of survival may be preferable to others.

For example, the problem of the commons, the problem of the carrying capacity of the planet strongly urges that if the human population growth of 80 million per year is permitted to continue to strain the earth's capacity to sustain it, the impact of that "problem" may well call for adaptive short-term "solutions" that reduce the altruistic side of the ratio to 20/80 or 10/90 either chemically or through a revision of the environmentally stable strategy—replicating on a global scale the urban situation just considered. This environmental challenge would be even more acute, however, because some 70 million of the 80 million new people per annum are born into societies that can least afford them. The other 10 million are born into societies that use a great deal of the earth's resources to sustain a much smaller population growth at higher standards of living. Under these sorts of conditions, where many of the less developed parts of the commons have nuclear capacity, the new environmental challenge may present an external problem of such magnitude that it can only be solved by internal genetic adaptation to the changing survival needs.

Evolutionary ethics may well argue that altruism is more genetic than was previously thought. But this by no means argues for altruism's permanence. The adaptabilitiy that makes us what we are can also change us. If this change is an undesirable future for human nature—a lessening of altruism and a heightening of selfishness—then the onus lies much more on changing the nature of the environmental challenge than on altering the ethics of the individual. Our preaching has, for a second reason been misplaced for centuries. We keep trying to make the individual strengthen the bonds that tie the whole species together, and fail to stem the tide of environmental change that will weaken those bonds even more than distance, language, religion, and culture already do.

The genetic involvement in human altruism does not at all imply that altruism is a fixed part of human nature that will survive all challenges. Rather altruism as a social instinct strongly argues that both in animal and human behavior real altruism can be seen. In a little book first published in 1938, Warder C. Allee summarized the matter quite well. Because in his animal studies he had never found an asocial animal, he felt comfortable ascribing social character to the nonhuman world. In his conclusion he wrote:

> We have good evidence, then, that these two types of social or subsocial interactions exist among animals: the self-centered, egoistic drives, which lead to personal advancement and self-preservation; and the group centered, more or less altruistic drives, which lead to the preservation of the group....[25]

Altruism is a part of our evolutionary inheritance and can comfort those who tire of descriptions of human nature in constant negative terms. But an understanding of what we are actually describing provides more than a comfort that altruism has been there all along—it provides in addition a warning not to take it for granted. Such an understanding also stimulates a different sense of ethics—inductive rather than deductive—that warns of the price that may be paid for irrelevance.

NOTES

1. Rosalind Miles, *The Women's History of the World* (New York: Harper and Row, 1988).

2. Edward O. Wilson, *Sociobiology: The New Synthesis* (Cambridge, MA: Harvard University Press, 1975).

3. Garrett Hardin, "The Tragedy of the Commons--Adaptation of Address," *Science*, December 1968, vol. 162, pp. 1243–1248.

4. Garrett Hardin and John Baden, eds., *Managing the Commons* (San Francisco, CA: Freeman, 1977).

5. Project Hope pamphlet, circa 1979.

6. Cicero, *On the Commonwealth*, G. Holland Sabine and S. Barney Smith, trans. (New York: Macmillan, 1976), p. 129.

7. Ibid. See discussion in Brian R. Nelson, *Western Political Thought from Socrates to the Age of Ideology*, Second Edition (Englewood Cliffs, NJ: Prentice-Hall, 1996), pp. 81-83.

8. Edward O. Wilson, *On Human Nature* (Cambridge, MA: Harvard University Press, 1978), p. 45.

9. See Nicholas Wade, "The Struggle to Decipher Human Genes," *The New York Times*, March 10, 1998, p. B10.

10. This fact was ascertained on a personal visit in February 1998 to the Currumbin Sanctuary in Queensland, Australia where the Red-necked Pademelon, among hundreds of other animals and birds, is preserved. This sanctuary formerly protected birds alone. Now it provides a safe home for all endangered species, from very large emus to very tiny lizards.

11. Paul W. Sherman, "Nepotism and the Evolution of Alarm Calls, *Science*, vol. 197, 4310, September 23, 1977, pp. 1246–1253. Additional information may be derived from W. W. Hamilton, "The Genetical Theory of Social Behaviour," *Journal of Theoretical Biology*, vol. 7, 1, July 1964, pp. 1–51. A later echo of this, with a naïve acceptance of Herbert Simon's "docility" can be found in Susan Rose-Ackerman, "Altruism, Nonprofits, and Economic Theory," *Journal of Economic Literature*, vol. 34 (June 1996), p. 712. For the silly idea that altruism leads to a society wherein more people are willing to be led ("docility"), see Herbert Simon, "Altruism and Economics," *Eastern Economics Journal*, vol. 83 (Mayl 1993), pp. 159–160.

12. Glenn Zorpette, "Parrots and Plunder," *Scientific American*, vol. 277, 1, July 1997, p. 24.

13. L. Milne and M. Milne, "The Social Behavior of Burying Beetles," *Scientific American*, vol. 235, 2, August 1976, pp. 84–89

14. That is certainly not intended here. This dispute within biology is fully described in Roger D. Masters, "Is Sociobiology Reactionary? The Political Implications of Inclusive-Fitness Theory," *The Quarterly Review of Biology*, vol. 57, 3, September 1982, pp. 275–292.

15. Paul W. Sherman, "Nepotism and the Evolution of Alarm Calls," *Science*, vol. 197, 4310, September 23, 1977, pp. 1246–1253.

16. Richard Dawkins, *The Selfish Gene* (New York: Oxford University Press, 1976).

17. T. Clutton-Brock, M. O'Riain, P. Brotherton, D. Gaynor, R. Kansky, A. Griffin, and M. Manser, "Selfish Sentinels in Cooperative Mammals," *Science*, vol. 284, 5420, June 4, 1999, pp. 1640ff, cited in "En garde?" *The Economist*, vol. 351, 8122, June 5, 1999, p. 78.

18. B. Drummond Ayres, Jr., "Town Finds Solace in Act of Heroism," *The New York Times*, March 26, 1998, p. 21. For a broader scope endorsement of human altruism see a provocative little piece by Annie Murphy Paul, "Born to be Good?" *USA Weekend*, a small weekly magazine stuffed into the weekend copies of *The Detroit News and Free Press*, July 23-25, 1999, pp. 6–8. Ms. Paul is pointing in the correct direction, but she bases her ideas on "new scientific research," words that should raise caution flags in any thinker.

19. Robert A. Daniels, "Nest Guard Replacement in the Anarctic Fish *Harpagifer bispinis*: Possible Altruistic Behavior," *Science*, vol. 205, 4408, August 24, 1979, pp. 831–833.

20. Glenn Zorpette, "Parrots and Plunder," *Scientific American*, vol. 277, 1, July 1997, p. 24.

21. John Maynard Smith, "The Evolution of Behavior," *Scientific American*, vol. 239, 3, September 1978, p. 178.

22. Stuart A. Altmann, unpublished speech given at the University of Michigan, March 31, 1979, p. 23.

23. Richard C. Lewontin, "Adaptation," *Scientific American*, vol. 239, 3, September 1978, p. 215.

24. Bertrand Russell, *Philosophical Essays* (London: Allen and Unwin, 1966), p. 24.

25. Warder C. Atlee, *The Social Life of Animals*, revised edition (Boston, MA: Beacon, 1958), p. 212. First published in 1938 as *The Social Life of Animals*, then a revised edition was printed in 1951 under a new title: *Cooperation among Animals with Human Implications*. Title reverted to original in 1958.

Part II

Barriers to Altruism

A person can have a good deal of fun thinking about altruism, imagining different ratios and under what circumstances a specific person might be moved to altruism. Or, the subject can be serious if altruism is thought of as a genetic inheritance that the ancients called natural law or as a social instinct that moves people to social action or community involvement. Surprisingly, something so significant to human survival as this has barriers that prevent it from operating freely and functioning effectively.

What would stop a person from being altruistic, from being kind to another at some cost to the self? A traditional answer would be the Devil or more simply, sin. When Augustine talked about barriers or impediments that got in the way of the clear functioning of an individual's natural law, he certainly thought he was talking about sin, a topic that is quite fully discussed in chapter 10. Impediments to right action, or "sin," Augustine felt, necessitated God's gift of a political system because the state would maintain the social order necessary for the peaceful growth of the church. Without the gift of the state, Augustine argued, people would live in chaos, like savages, involved in a war of all against all that may have later stimulated Thomas Hobbes's description of the state of nature. To prevent that chaotic disorder and to provide the basis for civilization, Augustine argued, God gave the state to people so as to provide external sanctions that would create a civic order people could no longer provide, an external order that would override the barrier of this "sin."

When the subject of sin is thought about, it seems as though the essence of the word, its rock-bottom meaning, is selfishness. Certainly, selfishness is the opposite of altruism but you cannot say that it is a barrier. Selfishness is a bad response to the need of another. A fetter is a bind that slows down the altruism, impedes it, constricts it, and makes it far less than it easily could be.

In the following three chapters I do not discuss sin. That is for Chapter 10. Instead, I consider three interesting impediments: first, the addictive brain that interferes with decent behavior and seeks to destroy itself; second, the organization and rigidification of a person's inner life by religion or ideology that drives individual behavior along prescribed lines and allowing no others; and, third, the development of impossible goals that actually create an excuse for not trying.

These are some of the fetters of altruism. There may well be more.

Chapter 4

Altruism and the Addictive Brain

Previously, when considering the nature of the human actor, the discussion centered on locating altruism deep in human nature as a part of the genetic inheritance, as another way of describing natural law, and as an instinct toward socialness that cannot easily be denied. In this chapter, it is interesting to discuss how difficult it sometimes might be for a person to be altruistic, to act on the basis of his or her own natural law; to consider what might stand in the way, what might interfere with one's free will.

In this chapter, the nature of the human is explored by probing the complexities of brain biochemistry. This amateur exploration should not give the impression that all individuals are locked into predetermined behavior caused by chemical and electrical combinations in the brain. But it should mark that these things need to be considered in a different way. Dr. Robert Weinberg said it well:

> For the first time, we humans are reducing ourselves down to DNA sequences. Aspects of the human spirit that have hitherto been as awe-inspiring will be reduced to rather banal biochemical explanations, and that's not altogether heartening.[1]

This exploration can create an appreciation for the difficulties some of us have acting on the basis of our altruistic impulses from within. We are definitely not equal in this regard, and some have a much harder road to follow than others, and this needs to be understood.

This inquiry into the nature of brain activity was stimulated by repeated notices appearing in various journals, magazines, and newspapers about breakthroughs in brain biochemistry; how the newer understandings of how the brain works make older ideas lying at the base of psychiatry and psychology less valid because the concept of the singularity of the psyche or mind, or soul on which those disciplines rest withers as a result of the lessening of the mystery surrounding the complexity and multifaceted character of brain functions.

In particular, the concept of the brain as a black box in which stimulus is directly transformed into response gave way to an appreciation of the brain as profoundly involved in not only receiving and responding to stimuli from the outside, but also in determining response due to an inside preprogrammed "wiring" system and chemical interplay. If the genes determined that this individual should produce less or more of an enzyme necessary for the appropriate functioning of part of the limbic system's neurotransmitters, attempting to change that response by preaching to that individual is futile. Attempts to alter the nature of that individual presuppose a freedom to change, but even the strongest will to change has great difficulty fighting the opposing genetic or chemical preset. The only attempts to change behavior that have a chance of success need to recognize the basic genetic chemical environment as well as feedback loops that allow external environmental events a limited opportunity of shaping future chemical activity inside the brain–body combination. In short order, therefore, any idea of free will is challenged by a growing awareness that human behavior is in many respects far from being free. Even those behavior alterations resulting from external environmental events quickly develop an habitual response mechanism that cannot be described as free. The exception seems to be the potential existing in highly focused, faith-supported mental activity directed at specific physiological phenomenon such as cancerous tumors where patients by very positive thinking have brought about beneficial results, or Alcoholics Anonymous where chronic, obsessive drunkards have been able to live and cope without drinking for decades.

Even with this knowledge of the significance of environmental factors and the awareness of the importance of positive thinking as causes for changes in brain chemistry, it is still true that the individual actor may not be free to respond to those outside influences, or at least not fully. Work on genetics but more especially research on brain chemistry suggests at least a reevaluation of the understanding of the nature–nurture interplay in the shaping of human behavior. If human thinking and behavior are more the result of genes and chemistry than of environmental influences then we need to spend more time on genetics and biochemistry and less time on environmental factors in our search for understanding. In trying to understand the behavior of an actor, the emphasis shifts from environment or nurture to internal programming or nature as the primary variable.

This new appreciation in turn conflicts with deeply seated notions about human character and knowledge that we all share to some degree, notions that result from John Locke's *Essay on Human Understanding* in the 1690s. The idea of a blank page on which sensations write led to the idea of human perfectibility, to the panacea of universal education, to an overvaluing of literacy, and to ideological single-solutions to social problems. These false starts had to be replaced with a more complex comprehension of the nature of the human knower, or the nature of the brain. But this still was not enough.

We also needed to understand the notion of *will*. Presupposed in our human grasp of things is an idea of will that allows an individual some freedom of choice when facing a need for a decision created by a stimulus. The word *will* or the concept *free will* is the abstraction people give to an imagined process underlying the behavior of choice. Because people choose one direction over another it is imagined that the choice was free—that it could have gone either way. But, again, considering the chemistry involved, such a concept of freedom is impossible to operationalize and foolish to conceptualize. Why do I choose? Because in many instances I must in order to continue living without pain or with minimum pain, because in my internal brain world that I received genetically and that has been reinforced by environmental conditions, habits of thinking and responding persist that are at base chemical and electrical. My image of my own survival, unknowingly distorted by chemical and electrical interplay, demands behaviors that only appear to be the consequence of a freedom of choice. The absence of full choice does not imply an absence of freedom. It rather implies that much of what we thought was freedom was in fact predetermined. The freedom we have lies in understanding the process and then altering, if possible and desirable, that determining nature.

All of this complicated mental processing of information occurs in microscopic cells acting individually and/or in concert with others to produce behavior. Watching this process, one is filled with awe that it works at all. Considering the poor "wiring" present in the brain and the various things that can go wrong, it is astonishing that such behavior exists. In the discussion and descriptions that follow, the questions that are being asked are as follows: "Where in all this is the will?" More deeply: "Where in all this involvement of genes and chemistry is the I, the self, the ego that René Descartes was so pleased to find in his doubting? It isn't there. The "I" or the self is an abstraction very much like the concept "soul," and may stand for the same thing: the essence of the human individual, a nonempirical phenomenon spoken of as though it belonged in the world of sense. The difficulty here is that our brains are equipped to handle only one language—the language of existence. We think and speak as though everything is an object, verifiable by sense impressions. For the world of existence that is no problem, but for the world of abstractions, the world of essence, it is a large problem because, long ago, we made God or angels out to be things. Then we exacerbated the whole problem as primitive people in that we named the items of essence, sealing them in totally inapplicable clothing. Think of what happens when your child names the animals in the farmyard. With the name comes a personality ascribed to the animal. When market day comes selling the animal is like selling your child. When one names something, one clothes it. As Johan Huizinga wrote:

> To the primitive mind, everything that is capable of being named immediately assumes an essence, be it a quality, a form, or something else. They project themselves automatically on the heavens. Their essence may almost always (but not necessarily always) be personified; the dance of anthropomorphic terms may begin at any moment.[2]

If one wishes, one can do much the same thing and be considered a profound philosopher. Aristotle, for example, moved from individual essence, soul, to world essence or God; or George W. F. Hegel moved from an apparently different essence, reason, to a unifying World Reason or World Spirit. On the other hand, perhaps the strong desire to make Gods in the image of humans should be resisted, because the old arguments about the reality of universals lie in the wings awaiting the unwary.

Consider then the individual and the actual operation of the individual controller or regulator of behavior—the brain.[3] It is a collection of cells and chemicals interacting to bring about chemical events that communicate by means of neurons, cells that specialize in transmitting information. Neurons consist of a cell body connected to a long component called an axon. The axon branches out into a number of nerve endings that, in turn, make contact with other neurons. Information processing in the brain occurs by communication between these different neurons. Transmission from the cell along the axon to a nerve terminal occurs via a propagated wave of ion movements encouraged by enzyme activity, somewhat akin to the passage of electricity along a wire. The neurotransmitter, one of more than thirty such known messengers, or the chemical manufactured in the neuron and stored in vesicles in the cell, diffuses across a gap called a synapse to influence the firing rate or activity level of the nearby neuron. It is able to do this because a highly specific receptor site exists on the other side of the fluid gap; a large protein molecule embedded into the membrane of the receiving cell. A part of the receptor is shaped exactly like the molecule of the transmitter chemical. The fit is like a key into a lock and normally insures (if not blocked or altered) that the proper signal directs the appropriate cell. In other words the receptor recognizes the neurotransmitter, unlocks the door to the cell, and triggers a change through the passage of one or another ion across the neuronal membrane. This is the communication language of the brain. The receptor translates the transmitter signal into a physiological response like a muscle contraction or the release of a specific hormone. The changes in electrical charges in this chemical environment have either awakened a neuron or have turned it off. Sometimes the first transmitter wakes up a second messenger, and by means of this relay system a message is exploded across the receiving cell. By changing the ionic permeability of the cell membrane, the transmitters can either excite or inhibit further neuronal firing.

At this point in the normal sequence, enzymes in the receiving cell deactivate the messenger--making possible several hundred pulsing signals per second. The enzymes are stored on tiny organisms called mitochrondria whose genetic material is unlike ours but resembles those of viruses and bacteria. The deactivation of mitochondria or their absence can cause havoc in brain operations. This enzyme action can be influenced by psychoactive drugs but also by endocrine (peptide) hormones produced by the pituitary.

The axons appear to have slow and fast lanes for transmitter traffic. Very fast response time demands great speed as in the instant reaction to pain. Substance P moves in micro seconds to influence response. But the replenishment of Substance P may take place at a slower pace, with the transmitter moving between one and twenty centimeters per day. Some of these messengers are fairly simple, like the monoamines or the neuropeptide enkeflins, whereas some of the other neuropeptides are long chains of amino acids that convey complicated information and orchestrate thirst, memory, and sexual behavior. These differences in complexity exist despite the amino acid common origin of all neurotransmitters.

In order to maintain ion gradients and transmitter activity, the brain uses some 20 percent of the body's energy although comprising only 2 percent of body weight. Thinking may use more energy than running. Neurons can only metabolize blood glucose and the process is entirely dependent on oxidative metabolism. That is why if the supply of oxygen is shut off, consciousness disappears on average in about ten seconds. Of course, interrupting the glucose availability can have the same result.

Each neuron possesses the ability to manufacture one or more transmitters. Some neurons apparently can make only one, and for a long time it was felt that one transmitter per neuron was a reasonable expectation. This belief changed when it became obvious that some neurons could and did produce many transmitters. But if it is assumed for the moment that only one is manufactured by enzyme action per neuron, a typical chain of events can be described. Instead of looking at a very complicated Substance P, which is a pain transmitter found in the brain, spinal cord, and nerve endings and contains eleven amino acids, it is simpler to look at a monoamine like tryosine. Tryosine becomes L-dopa, which becomes dopamine which can remain in that chemical form or become norepinephrine. The transmitter can be stored in quantities of 10,000 to 100,000 molecules until needed. The three major monoamine transmitters are dopamine, norepinephrine, and serotonin.

In recent years, serotonin drugs have become superstars in the sense of treating everything from depression to overeating, but at considerable risk. Drugs like Prozac, Zoloft, Paxil, Elavil, Redux, Pondimin, and Clozapine flooded the marketplace as apparently magic solutions, only to be recalled or altered as the risks of their use became more apparent.[4] This caused a widespread rejection of the whole idea of taking pills to lessen the effects of depression and represented a renewal, perhaps brief, of the idea that depression is caused by social rather than chemical factors. At any rate, in 1995 a survey discovered that only 20 percent of interviewed psychiatrists thought that depressed people should be treated with antidepressants.[5] Despite the evidence, however, that depression can be triggered by adverse external events, the newer drugs, like Prozac, are called selective serotonin reuptake inhibitors, and their use in 1996 increased rather than decreased. Prescriptions for Prozac alone rose from 136,000 in 1990 to 2.5 million in 1996. Overall, for new chemical antidepressants, about 5.4 million prescriptions were written in 1996. These increases seem to come particularly from general practioners. Ironically, therefore, one can see a greater disdain for pill taking and a greater use of the pills, presumably not by the same people.[6]

Dopamine has also been interesting to study in this context of understanding how behavior can change or swing from selfishness to altruism because of commands from the brain. Dopamine is normally concentrated in the regions of the midbrain called substantia nigra and ventral termentum. Additionally, many dopamine axons extend to the forebrain where they regulate emotional response. Others terminate in a region near the center of the brain called the corpus striatum where dopamine controls complex movements. The degeneration of these corpus striatum fibers results in muscular rigidity and the tremors associated with Parkinson's disease.

When dopamine piles up in the basal ganglia (cerebrum) because some of the nerve cells have died, the supply of two other transmitters, acetylcholine and GABA, appear to be depleted. This new chemical environment seems to cause tryptophan to break down into quinolinic acid instead of serotonin, and the presence of the quinolinic acid as well as the lowering of the serotonin level causes trouble. Injecting quinolinic acid into the basal ganglia of laboratory rats in one study[7] produced symptoms of Huntington's disease—a progressive degenerative neurological disorder characterized by jerky movements, irritability, violence, and profound mental deterioration.

Of interest here, particularly to alcoholics, is the relation between alcohol consumption and the release of serotonin by the brain, and an abstinence from alcohol resulting in deep depressions of the serotonin presence.[8] Then, in addition, there is the relation between quinolinic acid and tetrahydroisoquinoline (THIQ)—the chemical compound produced in the brains of alcoholics by condensation reactions of endogenous catecholamines with acetaldehyde or formaldehyde (intermediaries in the metabolism of ethanol and methanol respectively). The increased amounts of dopamine inhibit appetite while the THIQ creates a very strong preference for ethanol in laboratory rats and in humans as a means of satisfying thirst and possibly as a chemical reward. In an example of how one chemical combination can block the use of another, the THIQs bind to receptor sites formerly used by the catecholamines and block cholamine utilization by the neurons. The THIQs are also stored in the amine vesicles of neurons. Because of the tetrahydroisoquinoline presence, many normal brain reactions are blocked involving many other very important neurotransmitters like serotonin for depression or vasopressin for learning retention. The ingestion of alcohol causes a serious perturbation therefore in the normal metabolism of biogenic amines, amino acids, cyclic nucleotides, cations, proteins, and other endogenous factors in the brain. In addition, the deficiency of catecholamines because of blocked receptor sites, specifically a deficiency of the transmitter norepinephrine, is also linked to depression. No wonder alcohol is understood to be a depressant. The presence of the dopamine in the tetrahydroisoquinoline chain based on laboratory evidence appears to be responsible for the decided preference for alcohol commonly described by alcoholics as cravings and a compulsion to drink. Similar phenomena are noticed in other addictions like the craving for carbohydrates caused by depleted fat cells resulting from reduced dietary intake, or the withdrawal symptoms associated with severe caffeine reduction. These are very different chemical interrelationships, but they demonstrate the identical point. The brain, not "knowing any better," demands for itself what is harmful to the whole. Overriding these brain demands is very difficult as any recovered addict will report. What normally happens in addictive behavior is that the brain demands, and the itch is scratched until it bleeds and then is scratched some more.[9] This seems unbelievable until you see an example of it; like a person with obvious advanced emphysema sitting in a restaurant with his oxygen canister and lighting a cigarette!

Alcohol's chain of development in the brain of an alcoholic (but not that of a normal drinker) is a separation into components favoring the manufacture and distribution of dopamine that becomes THIQ. In a very tightly controlled laboratory situation, a study demonstrated that plasma tryptophan in alcoholics was depressed by ethanol. In rats fed a similar diet to those of alcoholics, this plasma tryptophan deficiency crossed the brain blood barrier as a deficiency of tryptophan in relation to other amino acids, resulting in a brain deficiency of serotonin. This deficiency helped to explain the depressive consequences of alcohol visible in the Branchey study, and because serotonin is also associated with temperature regulation, sensory perception, and the onset of sleep, the effects of such a deficiency could be widespread and profound.[10]

Alcoholics who drink because they are depressed or because without a drink they cannot go to sleep are actually, sadly, ingesting more of the cause of their problem and none of its solution, because alcohol depresses and prevents a person from falling asleep. A destructive spiral is thus actively encouraged by the very brain or reason that should guide us to heaven, to use Plato's analogy.

Although a dopamine pile-up in one part of the brain causes problems, a deficiency can cause other behaviors normally associated with aging.[11] Greater difficulties in body movements, reflexive responses, and stamina are now relatable to dopamine deficiency. But chemical interactions are not that simple. It is comparatively easy to imagine that there is a level of dopamine that is consistant with normal behavior, and increases or decreases can thus cause behavior problems. But the interrelated character of brain chemistry suggests that the increase or decrease of dopamine can result in an increase or decrease in norepinephrine with corresponding implications for maintaining arousal, sleeping with or without dreams, and the regulation of mood in response to stimulus. Furthermore, the rise or fall in dopamine levels occurs in conjunction with other chemical changes such as the mentioned one of depressed serotonin caused by the falling off of the supply of its precursor, tryptophan. These complicated chemical environments can determine whether quinolinic acid or tetrahydroisoquinoline is made.

As if this much complexity were not enough, it appears that different regions of the brain respond differently to varying concentrations of the same chemical. In most areas of the brain enkephlins act as opiates in reducing the electrical activity of cells. Some people even want to call these sorts of transmitters the brain's reward system and apply it to the learning process. "Learn this and you will get a shot of pleasure" sort of thing—something that may work for some parts of the brain but not others—the same enkephlin acts as an analgesic (pain reliever) in the midbrain but as an overexciter in the hippocampus.

One area evidently much related to brain and body chemistry is the perplexing problem of severe premenstrual syndrome (PMS). PMS in severe cases was accepted by English courts as a defense in crimes where women were accused of murder by stabbing, by automobile, manslaughter, arson, or assault. The women were probationed on the assumption that 50 to 100_{mg} of progesterone would end the cyclical pattern of criminal and violent behavior that can peak just before menstruation and subside after menstruation has commenced.

There is more mystery about menstruation than one might think. Recent studies have indicated even less individual control over one's body. Published in *Nature* in March 1998, the senior researcher, Dr. Martha K.

McClintock, put forward a new report on menstrual synchrony that she had first observed in 1971. In the 1998 study, the University of Chicago team demonstrated the significance of pheromones in causing the menstrual cycles of women who work or live together to move toward occurring at the same time. Compounds swabbed from the underarms of young women at different times of the month can alter the length of other women's menstrual cycles, either compressing or expanding them in a predictable fashion. Nine women wore cotton pads under their arms for eight hours during distinct phases of their cycles. The pads were then cut into sections, treated with alcohol, and wiped under the noses of twenty other women every day for a month. The twenty women stated that they could actually smell nothing but the alcohol. Nor could they see anything. Pheromones are both odorless and colorless. The point is that under very controlled circumstances the body behavior of these twenty women began to change in predictable ways.[12]

In the literature on menstruation some one hundred fifty symptoms have been associated with the cycle of menstruation. The commonest listed were tension, anxiety, abdominal discomfort, breast discomfort, swelling in the fingers and legs, headache, dizziness and palpitations. Some women experience a very severe PMS whereas only 3 percent have none. Most are somewhere in between.[13]

The severe cases, approximately 2.5 percent of reproductive-age women, have cyclical symptoms resembling those of people with severe mental disorders. Actual study of the comparison is suggestive. Premenstrual changes characterized by a depressive syndrome may represent a mild manifestation of an affective disorder.[14] There also seems to be a high correlation between psychiatric crisis and paramenstruum.[15] This study found that of thirty-nine women admitted to a psychiatric facility during a previous eighteen month period, some 41 percent ($n=16$) had been admitted on the day before or on the day of the onset of menstruation. The evidence was clear enough to have PMS listed as a psychiatric disorder in 1987, suggesting strongly that PMS was caused by something emotional—initially caused, perhaps, by some psychic trauma that could be discussed and dismissed. New evidence surfacing in 1998, however, pointed to chemical causation in the brain—severe PMS resulted from different responses to normal hormone levels, specifically reactions to estrogen or progesterone.[16]

The data remain unclear, however, and there appears to be a greater willingness to criticize the data than to study the brain to see why progesterone works in some cases, but not in others, or why in some cases placebos appear to do more than the progesterone. The placebo success is sometimes used to mock the progesterone findings, but what actually seems to happen is that the belief in the placebo's efficacy stimulates the brain's production of endorphins that do the work of the real pill better than the pill. The failure to understand the significance of placebos and actual brain chemistry, or the chemical context for the power of faith and belief causes doubt to be raised where none should be.

Additional evidence that behavior can be caused by chemicals lie in the findings that higher levels of serotonin block fear-learning mechanisms. Rats taught to fear electric shock seem quickly to forget their lesson when serotonin is administered.[17] Low levels of the same chemical have been linked to depression, aggression, and impulsivity. The combination of these three factors can lead to suicide. What possibly happens is that there is a blocking of serotonin receptor sites by something similar enough to lock on in place of it or an actual lowering of serotonin by lowered amounts of plasma tryptophan entering the brain with other amino acids. Marked increases in urine levels of CSF 5 hydroxyindoleacetic acid (5-HIAA), a serotonin metabolite, indicated the presence of a carcinoid tumor,[18] whereas lowered levels were found to correlate significantly with human aggression and suicide.[19] At NIMH, Goodwin found that individuals with higher serotonin levels in spinal fluids scored lowest on aggression tests, and those with higher norepinephrine scored highest. He believes that any chemical controlling violent behavior works by suppressing either the part of the whole brain governing ritualistic and hierarchical aspects of life and/or the part that governs our emotions and altruistic feelings. And once in place these chemical changes normally affect a person for life.

All these data can be looked at from another perspective. Imagine that the behavior of the body is already headed in a negative death direction and that the mind has the power to reverse this direction if the depressive cycles of anxiety and fear can be eliminated. Although the importance of this can be exaggerated, its significance should not be ignored. Simply projecting images of something better for ourselves, an image of when we were healthy and well, the body often responds as though it is healthy and well. So beliefs can change behavior and play a significant role in the cure of bodily ills.[20] And new behavior can change brain chemistry. Research has shown that behavioral therapy that changes obsessive behavior also changes the brain chemistry that caused it in the first place. Brain-imaging techniques have been used at the UCLA School of Medicine to demonstrate this.[21]

Moreover, there is probably no greater medicine existing in the world today than altruism. Helping someone else, even in very small ways, is good therapy because the helping instances can be the happy visualizations and affirmations that can counter the negative effects of illness.[22] It seems that helping someone else is the first baby step toward a cure of a great many ailments. The self-help literature at the local bookstore is replete with examples; some difficult to believe. But this is an easy one to test. The next time feelings are depressed, or the brain tries to seduce you into the old obsessive patterns, get up, get out, and help someone. It works.

Where altruism might have come from is important to understand, but it is also very important to see that the genes pushing certain actions in the individual are pushing against strong barriers in some cases. We preach at human rationality supposedly "located" in the brain that, sadly, is often sadly unable to do what the preacher asks. It is not enough to look at genes or embedded natural laws. One must also consider the actor: who and what we are inside ourselves, whether in terms of genetic predisposition or brain chemistry. Our selves seem to be a summaries of processes that may be little more than sophisticated words to describe the internal programming Aristotle talked about when he took Plato's form out of the sky and placed it within the individual. The form (soul) he spoke of is more genetic and chemical than he thought, but it is nonetheless the multidimensional seed of what we can be.

NOTES

1. Robert Weinberg, quoted in Nicholas Wade, "The Struggle to Decipher Human Genes," *The New York Times*, March 10, 1998, pp. B9-10.
2. Johan Huizinga, *The Autumn of the Middle Ages*, R. J. Payton and U. Mammitzsch, trans. (Chicago: University of Chicago Press, 1996), pp. 237–238.
3. The next few paragraphs are indebted to Solomon Snyder, "The Brain's Own Opiates," *Chemical Engineering News*, vol. 75, November 28, 1977, pp. 30ff.
4. Michael D. Lemonick, "The Mood Molecule," *Time*, vol. 150, 13, September 9, 1997,pp. 75–82.
5. Carol Daniel, "Depressed? Just Pop the Prozak," *The New Stastesman*, vol. 126, 4352, September 19, 1997, p. 18.
6. Ibid.
7. *Science*, vol. 205, 31, August 1979, pp. 886ff,
8. Mim J. Landry, "Serotonin and Impulse Dyscontrol: Brain Chemistry Involved in Impulse and Addictive Behavior," *Behavioral Health Management*, vol. 14, 1, January-February 1994, p. 35.
9. For additional information see Gerald Cohen, "The Synaptic Properties of Some Tetrahydroisoquinoline Alkaloids,' Murry Hamilton et al., "Identification of an Isoquinoline Alkaloid After Chronic Exposure to Ethanol," and R. Myers, "Tetrahydroisoquinolines in the Brain: The Basis of an Animal Model of Alcoholism," in *Alcoholism: Clinical and Experimental Research*, vol. 2, 2, April 1978, pp. 121, 1133, and 145. For reports on caffeine see *Science News*, vol. 123, 7, February 12, 1983. For an unusual article on obesity and an awareness of brain and fat cell involvement see *Newsweek*, C, 24, December 13, 1982, pp. 84ff.
10. Ibid.

11. *Science News*, November 10, 1979, p. 325, reporting a study by Marshal and Berrios reported in *Science*, October 26, 1979.

12. Natalie Angier, "Study Finds Signs of Elusive Pheromones in Humans, *The New York Times*, March 12, 1998, p. 18.

13. Van die Redaksie, *South African Medical Journal*, vol. 60, 23, December 1981.

14. Jean Endicott et al., *American Journal of Psychiatry*, vol. 139, 4, April 1982.

15. Abramowitz et al., *American Journal of Psychiatry*, vol. 139, 4, April 1982.

16. Dr. Peter J. Schmidt et al., *New England Journal of Medicine*, cited by Jane E. Brody, "Study Challenges Idea of PMS as Emotional Disorder, *The New York Times*, January 22, 1998, p. 1ff.

17. Trevor Archer, *Journal of Comparative Physiological Psychology*, vol. 96, 3, 1982, pp. 491–516.

18. "Hydroxyindoleacetic acid," *Everything You Need to Know about Medical Tests*, Annual (Springhouse, PA: Springhouse Corp., 1996), p. 579.

19. Brown GL; Ebert MH; Goyer PF; Jimerson DC; Klein WJ; Bunney WE; Goodwyn FK, "Aggression, Suicide, and Serotonin: Relationships to CSF amine metabolites, *American Journal of Psychiatry*, vol. 139, 6, June, 1982, pp. 741–746.

20. Herbert Benson, "Are You Thinking Yourself Sick?" *The Family Circle*, vol. 109, 5, April 2, 1996, p. 28.

21. Josie Glausiusz, "The Chemistry of Obsession," *Discover*, vol. 17, 6 June 1996, p. 36.

22. Ibid.

Chapter 5

Rigid Religious and Ideological Organizations

A second barrier to a freely acted out altruism is the kind of organized concepts and generalizations that creates a canonical significance to the body of thought in which one is supposed to function. Religions and revolutionary ideologies are examples of this barrier. It is not necessarily a religion such as Christianity or Islam or Judaism or the ideas of a Karl Marx that is the problem. Indeed, part of what religion does is absolutely superb—stimulating the composition of inspiring music and the construction of beautiful cathedrals that lift the soul away from the mundane to the spiritual. The most beautiful music and architecture is that associated with religion. But although the music and the buildings free the human spirit and allow it to soar without restraint, the revolutionary ideology can reconnect the individual to the dream of universal equality and community harmony. That ideological dream is powerful, and so is the religious music or the architecture of the world's great churches. The problem arises when the religion or ideology is institutional-ized, thus the freedom to soar or dream is no longer valued, even though leaders say it is.

What they say, however, is not what they do. What they do, and do very well, is to demand a freezing of new thought as orthodoxy is established by the "priests" and "priestesses" of the organization. This problem is widely perceived. The first two sentences of the 1992 book, *Toxic Christianity*, by author-psychologist Paul DeBlassie III, reads as follows: "Toxicity is a state of soul sickness that develops whenever individual growth and development is thwarted. Christianity becomes toxic as it is rigidly institutionalized."[1] Alison Luterman wrote "Is it OK for me to love Jesus but not be Christian?"[2] Individuals caught in the web of organized religion or ideology have lost their ability to think for themselves, and they are unaware that something precious has been left behind. Free thought is understood as the danger, not its suppression.

The freedom to think for oneself is exchanged for the dubious advantage of belonging. Any overt sign of free thought is first discouraged by edict and peers, then, if that does not work, the dissident is made to undergo a public confession. As a last resort, the person is evicted as a terrible heretic. If there is a state power behind the religion or ideology, the expulsion is accompanied by torture, imprisonment, and often death.

Examples are easy to find. The Inquisitions in the European 1200s illustrate a case where Christians persecuted other Christians for profit in the name of keeping pure the holy church. Pope Innocent IV in his papal bull *Ad extirpanda* in 1252 authorized torture during questioning. Goal? Preserving the church organization from challenging questions being raised at that time. Stalin successfully pushed torture through a Politburo meeting in 1934 for much the same reason: preservation of the leadership and organization called the Communist Party of the Soviet Union that he controlled.

Obviously, religion and ideology are not the only examples that could be brought forward; any significant freezing of thought will do—the social mores among the *haut monde* or *haut ton*, for example, or a country club that holds members to a line of behavior not their own, or any other tight organization of people like the military that spends much of the "boot camp" or "basic training" time removing all visible signs of independent thinking on the part of the new recruits.

This freezing of thought replaces individual thinking, and the absorption of the person into the religion or ideology is the replacement of individual thinking by the particular group-think. During the Korean War, such changes were often called brainwashings, but normally such pejoratives are not used to describe the process.

Altruism, as has been seen, is a possibly genetic survival instinct that ancients called natural law, an instinct that pulls the individual toward the social or community aspects of life. One would think, then, that absorption into the group would fit altruism like a glove. But that is not true. What happens is that the social or community ambience in which altruism or other virtues can be exercised is fundamentally altered. It is shrunk to the size of the significant group. Altruism is thought of only for the group, the party, or the church. Instead of helping widows and orphans in general, one helps only those widows and orphans in the church. The benefits of the ideology are also curtailed to those in the group or to those who convert. The dictatorship of the proletariat is supposed to eradicate everyone else, everyone not a proletarian. If this should happen, the original purpose of the organization, bringing something of benefit to the whole society would be lost, and interpreters would scramble to pretend that only members of the church are the whole world mentioned in John 3:16, or that the proletariat really includes everyone. Far too much time is spent preserving the organization, and far too little time is spent preserving the message that was originally the reason for the organization's existence.

Actually, the aim of those in charge of the organization is no longer to live or act virtuously, but to preserve the organization above all else. It is an unrecognized Machiavellian morality that sustains organizations, wherein whatever is good for the continued existence and prospering of the organization is deemed good, and whatever works to reduce the life of the organization is therefore evil no matter what happens to the individual in the process. Examples include the Roman Catholic complicity in the Holocaust in the 1940s and the Russian Orthodox Church remaining silent under communist control during the terrible 1930s when a holocaust of a different nature occurred among millions of Ukrainian farmers.

How can altruism be organized, how can it be represented by an organization? How can it function for an abstraction like religion or ideology when it is so closely tied to the moral consciousness of a particular, discrete human? The answer is difficult because the question is faulty. It is the individual who is organized and who is taught to believe that the morality of the organization should be and is his or her own morality. But an organization does not exist. Those who imagine that it does are deeply within the old error called *realism* wherein the reality of universals (abstractions) was affirmed. It was Aristotle, and particularly Aristotle as filtered through the Muslim Arabs of North Africa in the late Middle Ages that put an end to realism, or seemed to, because as Johan Huizinga wrote, realism was inherent to the whole European culture and not simply relevant to theology and philosophy. And this was true, he said, because realism is a primitive mode of thought and to the primitive mind, everything that is capable of being named immediately assumes an essence, be it a quality or a form that is projected automatically on the heavens. This essence is almost always (but not necessarily always) personified, and the dance of anthropomorphic terms begins.

> All realism in the medieval sense is ultimately
> anthropomorphism. If the thought that ascribes
> an independent essence to an idea wishes to
> make it visible, there is no other way except
> through personification.[3]

This is where symbolism and realism turn into allegory. In the process, the symbol is exhausted, a passionate cry is transposed into a grammatically correct sentence, and "the idea remains forever effective and unreachable and, though spoken of in all languages, inexpressible."[4] Unless one wants to think in this primitive, medieval fashion, which treats abstractions as real things, one is forced to conclude that only sensible objects exist, and among them individual people, people who have agreed to adopt a morality of an abstraction that does not exist; the organization, religion or ideology, that they have joined.

This does not mean that individuals are or should be isolate, or that alienation is a marvelous phenomenon. Each person can be a microcosmic, self-controlling whole system within larger social wholes rather than a pasted together collection of parts such as mind and body or soul and body. The brain, the center of consciousness and coordination, is as much a part of the body as the arms or legs. Abstractions such as "mind," "reason," or "soul" result from a misunderstanding of self-consciousness and a desire to treat essence as existence. And, like the sustaining earth itself, people have vital dependencies outside their individual selves such as each other, the world of nature, and a power greater than themselves called God, Gaia, Allah, or still different names by others. As individuals should not be isolate so also should they not be lost within an organization. A human is not a termite. Walking the wide path between these extremes is the goal.

Everyone who belongs to either a religion like Christianity or a revolutionary ideology like Marxist socialism does not lose the sense of individual morality within the whole. Most apparently do, but exceptions exist, and they stand out as almost weird compared to others in the same group. Some examples include Mother Teresa who personified altruism in India; Eduard Bernstein, the great Marxist revisionist who sought to reinstate the purpose of Marxist socialism; Francis of Assisi who cut to the love and sharing heart of Christianity. This does not mean that Christianity and revolutionary Marxism are polar opposites. In many respects, they are very similar because both seek to express the rhythms of the universe and a reverence for life. Evolving religions emerged from the human need to express those concepts spiritually and to show how it all leads to a serene pleasantness; revolutionary ideologies arose from the frustrations created by religion's failure to bring on that Kingdom of Heaven.

The early days of a religion's development (or that of an ideology) must have been exciting. Creating the explanation of life's beginning and of human relationships as the work and story of the universal power we normally call God, and indicating where it all was going were probably exhilarating, cosmic leaps into invisible worlds. Unfortunately, that exciting creativity was replaced by a stultifying orthodoxy and by the explication of sacred texts in both religion and revolutionary ideology.[5] Orthodoxy ended the toleration of ambiguity, the acceptance of slight or even great differences in exactly what one or others believed. For example, in religion, does it make a difference if a person believes that Jesus was the created son of God rather than a coeternal part of God? Before orthodoxy it did not matter. Perhaps, more attention was paid to whether a person acted like a Christian rather than that he/she believed "properly." Orthodoxy forces attention to the beliefs, the rituals, the creeds as though this is virtue, as though this is Christianity. But believing in altruism does not make one altruistic.

The same is true with revolutionary ideology. The worst examples of

Marxism in this regard are the Russian 1930s when millions of people were needlessly and deliberately killed in the name of the communism that sought to liberate them. Orthodoxy within the Communist Party of the Soviet Union began in 1921 at the Tenth Party Congress with the prohibition on factionalism passed by that Congress. Dissenting from the views of the top leadership was made punishable by expulsion from the party, similar to the "America—love it or leave it" approach used in the late 1960s when Americans who supported the Vietnam War felt quite orthodox. Maintaining the organization was paramount. After 1921, communism became whatever the top people said it was, and as the years passed that increasingly meant whatever Josef Stalin said. Communism or socialism is whatever he said it was. Like the Pope for Catholic Christianity.

Imagine Christian Crusaders on the way to Palestine raping Christian women in Constantinople. A communist death squad night after night bringing truckloads of people to Kurapaty Forest to murder them over ditches to facilitate their burial. Christians in Chiapas, Mexico murdering men, women, and children. In Guatemala, raping students. In Cambodia, shooting old women for being slow. In Hungary, burning down Gypsy housing. In America, drowning one's own children. In Ukraine, stealing the seed grain to cause massive starvation. In Vietnam, killing men, women, and children on the whim of a mistaken man in Washington DC. In China, killing thousands in order to subdue Tibet.

The list could go on but it need not. The point is that both religion and revolutionary ideology can so stifle one's intrinsic sense of altruism that it is hardly visible at all. There was no toleration of ambiguity in this evolved organizational orthodoxy. Early Christian dissenters like the Donatists in North Africa were violently put down as soon as the Christian church was given the power by the state to do so. Or Muslim women and girls were raped by Orthodox Christian Serbian soldiers because they had military power behind them. And because the people who ruled the church were not necessarily religious or were religious in a nationalistic and narrow sense, the rules that had to be followed and the guidelines for morality were rules that made sense for the preservation of the ruling class, not for the good of the members of the church, or for those outside that Jesus came to call. This phenomenon is still very visible in Latin America and elsewhere where the gap between rich and poor is enormous and the church officially sides with the rich while it serves the poor.

Religions or ideologies came to refer to one's own set of ideas and practices as truth. In ancient Russia, Nikon, the church leader at the time of Peter the Great's father could not even change the number of fingers extended when one crossed oneself without creating enormous, bitter strife that lasted for centuries. The orthodoxy was too strong. He could not even correct the mispelling of Jesus's name. Nor, later, could anyone question Stalin without being arrested. Communist orthodoxy was no improvement. These frozen ideas became ritualized, habitual responses as the individual identified with the larger whole and trained his or her own thinking to parallel that of the organization. Individuals who stood up to dissent were treated at first with condescension, even pity at their erroneous thinking. Persistence in dissenting, however, brought an ever increasing harshness from the top of the organization.

An example of this frozen wasteland is not hard to find. In terms of revolutionary ideology the German Social Democrats (SPD) in the nineteenth century were like a church, a religion. The writings of party theoreticians became the prayerbooks of the movement, and the ideology

> became a set of slogans, a set of war-cries—a litany intoned again and again, drummed into the listeners' heads at meetings and rallies. They always used the same phrases, fortified only by invective. It became language no longer for thinking, but for arousing. What is more, regardless of its doctrines, the Marxist movement attracted large masses of workers because it gave them an exciting feeling of self-liberation and self-education: it gave them pride in participation, solidarity in defying their bosses, and a great sense of camaraderie.[6]

Granted, the SPD was not a church, but it certainly behaved like one. It labeled as heretics those who questioned the accepted "Marxist" dogmas, or "in a more benign mood, suggested that they had not sufficiently mastered Marxist theory, and in general relied on discipline and obedience for its continued existence as a militant movement."[7]

Thus, both communism and Christianity can be considered religions with differing views of salvation, sin, redemption, and spiritual life. They can even sound similar when referring to the "afterlife," which for Christians would be the apocalypse and heaven and for ideologues the Revolution and socialism, meaning approximately the same thing. Louise Michel, an anarchist involved in the Paris Commune of 1871 and a leader on the far left for the next twenty years, wrote in her memoirs about the approaching glorious revolution. She wrote:

> Then the great uprising will come. The rising of the people will happen at its appointed moment, the same way that continents develop. It will happen because the human race is ready for it. That uprising will come, and those whom I have loved will see it. O my beloved dead."[8]

This commonality of religion and revolution can be obscured through an emphasis on materialism rather than spiritualism in communism and by underscoring the privatized rather than socialized gospel in Christianity. If religion seeks only souls and communism only bread the two can stay apart. But neither can maintain the apartness for very long, Dostoyevsky's *The Grand Inquisitor* to the contrary notwithstanding. Why? Because there is an attracting bond between these two Western religions—a spiritual core in Marxism and a communism in Christianity that is quite visible in each. In Christianity a global implementation of the religion would result in a visible brotherhood or sisterhood under the fatherhood or motherhood of God, egalitarianism, love as the motivation for behavior, sharing as a way of life, peace, joy, happiness, and harmony in all relations—individual, community, and international. The ultimate goal, heaven, spiritualizes these desired earthly accomplishments and adds an eternal, blissful proximity to God. The chief beneficiaries of all this Christianity were supposed to be the very poor, the πτοχος, to use the ancient Greek word for the very low poor in Palestine, the very poor that the church normally neglects.

The implementation of Marxism seems very similar even though the descriptive words sound different. The socialized means of production will allow a disappearing proletariat to share the wealth capitalism has taught the workers how to produce. There will be an end to class and class conflict and there will be peace between individuals, communities, and nations. A world of brothers and sisters living in love and harmony will enjoy leisure, the satisfaction of need rather than payment for work, the sharing of the fruits of their labor necessary to their happiness, a fullness of life without alienation, and continuous progress. The implementation of Marxism sounds materialistic, but so does Christianity when it speaks of the Kingdom in this world rather than in the life after death. Both Marxism and Christianity have spiritual dimensions as well.

The sad fact is that both Christianity and Marx's ideology postpone altruism to the postapocalypse/revolution future. They act as though it is impossible in the present ambience, which has the effect of justifying selfishness because one is either a victim of sin ("I'm only human") or a victim of capitalism ("we do live in capitalism, so buy cheap and sell dear").

The clearest escape from this orthodoxy trap in Christianity has been liberation theology, a movement prominent in Latin America from 1960 to 1980 by Christians who expect the Kingdom of Heaven to appear on earth, as is said, emphatically, in the words of the Lord's Prayer "...Thy Kingdom come, Thy Will be done, on earth as it is in heaven." There is in both religions a childlike acceptance of the material possibility of that golden future, an acceptance that ignores all practical questions in the simple belief that a new day is coming. The question "How?" is answered with the smile of faith on the face of the believer, a smile that pities the questioner's lack of "understanding."

Many Roman Catholic nuns, priests, and occasionally bishops in Latin America between 1960 and 1980 were involved in what was called Liberation Theology, a this-world liberation movement that arose outside the church in Russia (revolutionary ideology), but also inside the church in Latin America (Liberation Theology). Priests in Russia did not join with but fought with Marxists, whereas common ground was often found in Latin America where it was discovered that Marxists and Liberation Christians were often seeking the same thing for the same people despite the fact that Karl Marx argued that religion was a social narcotic.[9] The Russian side emphasized the differences between the two ideologies, whereas the Latin American side stressed the similarities.

In Russia, during the period from 1890 to 1917, the Russian Orthodox church was already very old. It was begun in 988 by Prince Vladimir as an offshoot of the church in Byzantium, but by 1051 had become independent. Because it began in the Eastern Roman Empire where the emperor lasted until 1453, the orthodox church grew to maturity under the control of the prince. Caeseropapism the practice was called, caesar or king rules the church. In the Western Roman empire, in the ambience of no emperor for all intents and purposes in the Roman fifth and sixth centuries, the Roman Catholic church matured without political control and indeed imagined that it itself was a political power. Hence, the pope's medieval struggle with the kings of new states in France, Spain, and England that was called the Investiture Struggle. In the East, none of this happened and for centuries the church continued under state control with but infrequent attempts to pull the church away from materialism and property acquisition or out from under state control.

In the nineteenth century, this weakness of the Russian Orthodox church became more evident because the need for the church to participate in alieviating peasant slavery (serfdom) rather than participating in it ran squarely into the desires of the state to protect the status quo—the dominance and wealth of the landowners. Not too different from the position of the Latin American church hierarchy and popes as well in the period between 1960 and 1980. In the Russian case, the few priests who sought social action were quickly defrocked by church leaders, especially between 1905 and 1907. A less successful effort to accomplish the same thing occured in Latin America. Outside the church in both instances, a spirit of liberation ran high among so-called atheists and materialists. The liberation message, the altruism, was coming from a different source even though many still felt it should come from the church.

Vissarion Gigorievich Belinski, for example, rejected Russia's exploitative past history. In an 1847 letter to Nikolai Vasilyevich Gogol, Belinski wrote about the passivity of the Russian Orthodox Church. He told Gogol that "one cannot keep silence when lies and immorality are preached as truth and virtue under the guise of religion and the protection of the knout."[10]

Belinski argued that in his letter Gogol had recommended that in the name of Christ and Church the landowner should make even more profits out of serfs[11] and to abuse them more even though those peasants were the landlord's brothers in Christ,

> and since a brother cannot be a slave to his brother, he should either give them their freedom, or, at least, allow them to enjoy the fruits of their own labour to their greatest possible benefit, realizing as he does, in the depths of his own conscience, the false relationship in which he stands to them.[12]

Belinski argued that Gogol's position was certainly consistent with that of the Russian Orthodox Church, which had always served as the servant of despotism. But, Belinski asked of Gogol, why have you mixed Christ up in this? Belinski's point was that because the church was not living Christianity, Christ was not in the church, but outside it. Actually, he argued, a person like Voltaire was more a son of Christ than all the religious leaders of either East or West.[13]

Almost three decades after Belinski, Vera Figner, a revolutionary woman who became involved with the revolutionary organization, The People's Will, and with the assassination of Tsar Alexander II, wrote that she

> accepted the idea of socialism at first almost instinctively. It seemed to me that it was nothing more than a broader conception of that altruistic thought [about helping others less fortunate than she] which had earlier awakened in my mind.[14]

Vera wrote that Jesus had taught that self-sacrifice is the most supreme act of which a person was capable. The Gospels were the most authoritative source we knew, she said, not only because we were accustomed to seeing it as a holy book in childhood, but because of its inner spiritual beauty.[15]

Belinski's words, like Figner's, are often taken as atheism or as a secular religion. They would be more correctly seen as religion taken out of the church so that the core message was freed and thinking was once again individual.[16] However, people within the Russian Orthodox Church, the intellectuals putatively able to see both problems and potential solutions, opted for more of the old traditional ways rather than direct social action, signalling that peculiar blindness that affects so many religious people who drive to a rally for foreign Christian missions and drive through appalling poverty surrounding the church. They think to move their church out of the poor neighborhood instead of working within it.

Three such blinkered intellectuals were Vladimir Soloviev, Sergei Bulgakov, and Dmitri S. Merezhkovsky. They all wished to see significant reforms in the Russian Orthodox church, permitting the church to respond to outside challenges, but they could not comprehend a redemptive, social movement that was not at the same time a part of the organized Orthodox church. Like the people driving to the mission rally, the altruistic drive that should be individual had been given to an organization and only when that organization sanctioned the assistance to the nearby poor would such assistance be provided. Recall the Communist International and how obedience to this organization took precedence over loyalty to one's own country even when one's own country was invaded. In either case the phrase "selling one's soul" comes to mind.

Sergei Bulgakov, who had once been a Marxist, imagined that Russian Marxism was a perverted sort of negative Christianity, and although he thought that the socialist task arose from the church, Russian Marxism's divorce from the church and its move to atheism made it impotent in his judgment and unable to succeed,[17] instead of a different ideology on the same track that could be temporarily supported.

The Russian Orthodox Church fought capitalism not because capitalism was greedy, exploitative, and destructive of life and its environment, but as part of its long struggle to keep Russia from changing in the direction of the decadent West. Remaining within the traditional church, the "liberation theology" in Russia intensified the spiritual to escape the problem and to distinguish itself from the material form of liberation (socialism or social-democracy) and that religious intensification led to apocalypticism, even further away from the masses. For example, Vladimir Ern and Valentin Sventsitski, two of the founders of the short-lived Brotherhood of Christian Struggle in 1905, argued for a two-stage revolution. The first stage was the revolution of secular socialism. Although they felt that the first stage would be nurtured by the spirit of Christ, Ern and Sventsitsky felt that such a spirit could not be acknowledged by atheistic socialists. This state, therefore, had to be overcome rather than influenced by Christians to make room for the Brotherhood's apocalyptic second stage, which resembled the Age of the Spirit as foretold by Joachim of Fiora at the end of the twelfth century. The goal of this second revolution, the spiritual one, was a sobornal (holy or sanctified) community[18] and, of course, the Russian nation would play a leading role in this revolutionary apocalypse.[19] This second stage, therefore was as much secular as spiritual as religious in the sense that Alekséi Stepánovich Khomiakóv, the founder of Slavophilism, meant that second revolution to mark the triumph of Russian (Greek) Orthodoxy over Catholicism and Protestantism in the West. The glorious day of universal salvation became a parochial victory. So although the first stage sounded as though it might work toward the solution of social problems, the second clearly ignored them or saw them solved as part of the victory of Orthodoxy. Nor was it ever explained properly how in that first or second stage an equalizing redistribution of wealth could take place in an autocracy. The closest may have been the concession by Sergei Bulgakov that the social democrats offered "a vision of a *sobornal* future, a 'union in love and freedom,' which corresponded to age-old yearnings of Russia's people."[20] The problem for Bulgakov was that socialism promised a secular utopia that it could not produce. Political means, in his judgment, simply could not lead to transformed humans.[21] However correct (or incorrect) he may have been, he could not see how similar the rejected position was to his own. Because his was spiritual he thought it different. The socialist utopia was also a spiritual conception of the human transformation, but the ideologues could not admit this. Vladimir Soloviev, Bulgakov's mentor, had taught that the human transformation into what Soloviev called Godmanhood was a totally spiritual reunification between God and the human race that was the goal of creation and all of history.

Soloviev was a mystical idealist who argued that the created world had fallen away from God and now comprised hostile and separate parts, an alienation that Soloviev considered sin. This alienation had to be overcome and the way this was accomplished was through Jesus Christ. Christ, to Soloviev, was God-man who represented a divine–human unity, a unity that had to be replicated cosmically for world alienation to be overcome.[22] Assisting the world to accomplish this cosmic theosis was something he called a world soul, a female aspect of the essence of God that Soloviev called Sophia. Sophia appeared to Soloviev occasionally in his dreams, often enough, however, to become the focal point of his religious striving. She became the intermediate goal in the sense that serving her meant working for the spiritual salvation of the world, resulting in

> a religious love for the world and mankind in its
> sacred, potentially divine and beautiful primary
> nature. This leads to the striving to transfigure
> and deify the world so that its actual condition
> should correspond to its essence as conceived by
> God.[23]

Although such thinking could have motivated some fine altruism, the individual was lost in a cosmic vision, and pulled away from action. Changed behavior was prevented by linking Soloviev's philosophical idealism with the moral idealism of the revolutionary populist tradition in Russia,[24] which pulled the individual back into tradition, status quo, and the fear of Western ideas.

After the 1905 "revolution" in Russia, Dimitri S. Merezhkovsky summed up this idiocy by calling for a new but religious revolution that would usher in the millennium when the sky would caress the earth and bring forth a new sky and a new earth.[25] How far from altruism can one get? It was evidently easier to work for a sexual union of earth and sky than it was to get into villages and streets to bring about real changes for real people.

There was no action, of course. The internal force that pushes one into altruistic activity, helping others at some cost to oneself, was stultified by religion's tendency to imagine that the material is transcended by the spiritual, that action can be replaced with piety. They missed the point entirely. Jesus said I was hungry and you fed me, thirsty and you gave me drink; a stranger and you took me in, naked and you clothed me, sick and you visited me, in prison and you came to me. Then the righteous said, when did all this happen? When did we see you hungry or thirsty? And he answered, inasmuch as you have done it to the least of these my brothers you have done it to me.[26]

Right.

A different response was visible in Latin America after Pope John 23rd's encyclicals *Pacem in Terris* and *Mater et Magistra* were published in the early 1960s and after the Second Vatican Council that met from 1962 to 1965. The new emphasis coming from the top of the Roman Catholic Church was on working for peace and justice and greater religious freedom, and finding more areas of cooperation with other ideologies. Although the academic dialogue between Marxism and Christianity began in Europe, it was to find its greatest practical application in Latin America where already existing priestly activism was now endorsed, given a theological foundation, and a name by Gustavo Gutierrez' book *Theology of Liberation*. It quickly became clear that this was not simply an academic or theoretical exercise. The men and women of this new movement, which included some Protestants, began to use their churches as agents of social transformation. In other words they began to apply individual standards of altruism from the very institution that had previously strangled it.

Richard Shaull, a Protestant, described this Latin American, leftist Christianity as a struggle for humanization.[27] Another Protestant, Jurgen Möltmann, saw this new Christianity as a revolutionary force for transforming the world, a movement that did not dare to dream away about eternity while real people suffered hunger and cold. Möltmann called the Kingdom of Heaven as preached and practiced by Jesus a realizable possibility on earth.[28] And this Kingdom of Heaven is about bread as well as spirit. For example:

> Christ has come not only to liberate [people]
> from [their] sins. Christ has come to liberate
> [them] from the consequence of [their]
> sin...prostitution, racial discrimination...money
> concentrated in a few hands, land possessed by
> a small number."[29]

These words by Bishop Antonio Batista Fragoso were a deliberate use of Christianity for social as well as spiritual ends. The theology of liberation that blossomed so brilliantly and then faded from the scene represented the closest the Christian church has ever come to freeing altruism so that it could function as an instrument of morality.

Gustavo Gustierrez, for another example, wrote that sinning was refusing to love one's neighbor and if you did not love your neighbor you did not love God. Behind unjust structures (like private property) lay a willingness by Christians and non-Christians to reject God and neighbor.[30] Bishop Dom Helder argued that the institutionalized poverty of the masses represented a significant and fundamental disorder in creation that interfered with God's special gifts that permit humans to transform the world. The structured injustice so visible in the Third World fostered by an international economic colonialism was a permanent disenfranchisement enforced particularly by the United States and the Soviet Union as it then existed. Humans created in the image of God could not realize that image because of the unjust use of power (violence) that was directed against the masses. It was necessary to use violence on their behalf.[31]

This acquiescence to violence could have led to enforced altruism in the name of Jesus, an unhappy combination at best, but before this could really occur the church hierarchy did its level best to combat it in the interests of the status quo. What the church had blessed in the beginning was now feared as a disruptive force. From Pope John Paul through the archbishops and most of the bishops the pressure was on for conformity to the old days when nothing was done. The altruism dried up considerably and the organization of the church on the side of the wealthy was preserved.

Similarly in the revolutionary ideology known as Marxism the most significant breakout was nearly universally condemned; in large part because it upset a fragile unity of the Marxist movements in the Second International (1889–1914) in that it brought the struggle between reform and revolution out into the open. The organization was deeply split on the issue because the delegates came from countries with widely differing cultures. In the 1890s, for example, most of the workers had the vote in Britain, Germany, and France and they were also beginning to achieve significant gains through unionization. In Britain the Labour Party emerged in 1893 as a political representative for Labour in the House of Commons. The working class had several tools it could now use to achieve gains for itself. These delegates were for reforms, and most definitely not for revolution. Why would they seek to overthrow the government they were becoming a part of? Why overthrow an economic system they were beginning to manipulate? In Russia and eastern Poland, however, none of this was true. They could not be for reform because there were no levers of reform in Tsarist absolutism. It had to be revolution.

But delegates meant different things by that word.

Karl Kautsky, for example, until 1917 the editor of the party journal *Neue Zeit,* stood for a Marxist orthodoxy that included an acceptance of surplus value; capitalist contradictions; the increasing misery of the proletariat; the dropping of the small capitalists into the ranks of the proletariat, victims of the class division widened by monopolization and growth of big business; and the progressive socialization of the working force. Even though he believed all this, his notion of revolution was based on an evolutionary model. Working for the revolution meant working for the proletariat, but never to the extent of increasing the power of the bourgeois state. This limited the scope of what the workers' representatives could accomplish in parliament because while Kautsky was for parliamentary activity on behalf of the workers, he refused to permit that activity if it mean cooperating with bourgeois parties.

This restricted the effectiveness of the parliamentry group in bringing about desirable social change that would benefit the poorer classes. Kautsky, nonetheless, had a strong faith that the future would be socialist after a majority of the people had been won over. His workers' state would come about by peaceful evolution, never by the violence that accompanied the dictatorship of the proletariat in Lenin's Russia in 1917 and 1918. Although Kautsky believed that a disciplined and unified proletariat was necessary to achieve a socialist future, it would accomplish this through democratic means. The revolution became synonymous with socialism rather than the means of achieving it.

This reformist strain was dominant but it was couched in revolutionary terminology that seemed to satisfy both reformists and revolutionists in the organization. Both sets of delegates sang the same songs and shouted the same slogans. The songs and slogans tended to be revolutionary and were interpreted differently as they were used. This delicate balance was shattered by Eduard Bernstein (1850–1932). Although a German and a prominent member of the SPD, he was almost as much influenced by England as he was Germany. He had lived there for several years. He became very close to Friedrich Engels before Engel's death in 1895. Bernstein was also influenced by the reformist socialist group, the Fabian Society. Beginning in 1896 with articles published in *Neue Zeit,* he radically criticized Marxism and stirred up controversy and condemnation within party ranks and from other sections of the Second International. In 1899, he summarized his ideas in a book called *Die Voraussetzungen des Sozialismus und die Aufgaben der Sozialdemokratie.* The title in English is much shorter: *Evolutionary Socialism* and has remained in print for a century.

Bernstein had no intention of destroying Marxism; he just wanted to purge it of things Marx had been mistaken about, things that history had revealed to be untrue. First, Bernstein attacked the general reticence about discussing the socialist future as an attitude that led to the idea that after capitalism there would be a sudden (magical) leap into a socialism that would solve all problems. Second, he challenged the idea that capitalism was in its death throes. In the 1890s it was obvious that capitalism had a long ways yet to go. Third, he argued against the notions of economic determinism and narrow class understanding. He wanted to free proletarian thinking from the Marxist orthodoxy that would not allow it to see the world as it really was. Indeed, he argued, that Marx himself did not see the world correctly, but read it through the spectacles of Hegelian philosophy. Bernstein put it in the metaphor of a construction site. Marx, he said raised a mighty building (Marxism) within the framework of the scaffolding he found already existing (Hegelianism a la Feuerbach), and in its erection he kept strictly to the laws of scientific architecture so long as they did not collide with the conditions which the construction of the scaffolding prescribed, but he neglected or evaded them when the scaffolding did not allow of their observance. Where the scaffolding interferred, Marx changed the building rather than adapt the scaffolding. Bernstein said that it was his judgment that the scaffolding should have been changed so that the building could grow straight and true. But since that had not happened, many things in the building were not right.[32]

For example, small capitalists were still healthy, land ownership seemed to be moving into more hands, the middle class was not dying out, and the proletariat was not becoming poorer, but actually was better off than it had been a few years ago. The dictatorship of the proletariat, he thought, was insufficiently democratic. And so forth—a real critique that might have destroyed the rigid orthodoxy, but like the challenge of Protestantism in the early sixteenth century, the revision affected only a few. The mainstream reacted, retrenched, reformed slightly, and then continued just as rigidly as before. As the organization crumbled during World War I, the mainstream shifted eastward and the Bolshevik success in taking power in 1917 made them the mainstream. As a result an orthodoxy that championed a violent revolution was preserved.

The telling of this long story allows several things to become clear. Orthodoxy, whether in religion or ideology, is a rigidifying of ideas that supplants rather than nurtures the natural altruism of its members whose kind feelings for others should have been enhanced by their membership in the organization. Creativity was stifled, scientific curiosity was deadened, and adventuresome individuals were either killed or despirited.

What is insufficiently remembered by students of history is that today's orthodoxy was yesterday's search for an impossible world. This is particularly true where the impossible world sought was too grand in scope and attempted to explain everything. Compromises, like cheating at solitaire, become difficult to stop once begun. And the new world such compromises create is a copy of the old that was overthrown.

Two behavioral morals emerge from this study. First, tolerate ambiguity in others to the highest degree possible and seek as few definitions as possible.

It is far more important to implement God than to define God, and it is far more significant to *live* sisterhood or brotherhood than to write about it. There is, particularly in the Western world, an incredibly seductive addiction to definition and abstraction that allows mental gymnastics to replace actual exercise. Seek commonalities rather than differences and recognize the right of others to differ from yourself.

Two, keep method and goal coinciding so that the goal becomes the method and the method the goal in a revolutionary praxis that does not await some distant millennium for the fulfillment of the dream. Implement it now, where you stand by seeing that the goal is the pathway. The steps one takes will be small, but they will be steps.

Small, incremental steps can lead to structural transformations that frontal assaults by organizations have never accomplished.

NOTES

1. Paul DeBlassie, *Toxic Christianity* (New York: Crossroad, 1992), p. ix.

2. Alison Luterman, "Jesus Incognito," *The Sun*, January 1999, p. 28.

3. Johan Huizinga, *The Autumn of the Middle Ages*, Rodney J. Payton and Ulrich Mammitzsch, trans. (Chicago, University of Chicago Press, 1996), pp. 237–238.

4. Ibid., p. 238.

5. The Council of Nicea in 325A.D. is generally considered the beginnings of Christian orthodoxy, because it was then and at later councils that specific formulae were adopted about the nature of the Trinity, the two natures of Jesus, as well as the specific books permitted into the canon called the New Testament. The rise of orthodoxy with respect to Marxist ideology can be traced to a period shortly before the death of Marx in 1883, and indeed during the 1890s when Bernstein was tepidly condemned, but for its full expression it should probably wait until Lenin began the Third International in 1919 and insisted that only parties loyal to Leninism could be members of the Comintern.

6. Alfred G. Meyer, *The Feminism and Socialism of Lily Braun* (Bloomington: Indiana University Press, 1985), p. 42.

7. Ibid., p. 85.

8. Bullitt Lowry and Elizabeth Ellington Gunter, eds. and trans., *The Red Virgin—Memoirs of Louise Michel* (University, AL: University of Alabama Press, 1981), p 196.

9. Clifford Green, "Karl Marx, Religion, Social Narcotic and Reactionary Ideology," in Johnson, Roger et al., *Critical Issues in Modern Religion* (Englewood Cliffs, NJ: Prentice-Hall, 1973), p. 143.

10. Vissarion Grigor'evich Belinsky, *Selected Philosophical Works* (Moscow: Foreign Languages Publishing House, 1956), p. 536.

11. A serf is a peasant slave. See Chaper 8 for a clear description.

12. Ibid., p. 538.

13. Ibid., p. 539.

14. Vera Figner, *Memoirs of a Revolutionist* (New York: Greenwood, 1968), p. 164. Also, for the religious mood of the Zurich group of Russian female medical students in the mid-nineteenth century, the group that included Vera Figner, see Barbara Alpern Engel, *Mothers and Daughters: Women of the Intelligentsia in Nineteenth Century Russia* (Cambridge: Cambridge University Press, 1983), p. 141.

15. Barbara Engel, ibid.

16. Stepping from a church to a revolutionary ideology however, is no help because in fact one is stepping from one religion to another. Or, possibly, from one revolutionary ideology to another.

17. Christopher Reed, *Religion and Revolution in Russia 1900–1912* (New York: Harper & Row, 1980), pp. 61–62.

18. The Russian word *sobor* means church or cathedral, whereas the intensified word *sobornost* has a variety of meanings, but usually refers to a religious collectivity or community as understood by Khomiakóv.

19. George F. Putnam, *Russian Alternatives to Marxism: Christian Socialism and Idealistic Liberalism in Twentieth-Century Russia* (Knoxville, TN: University of Tennessee Press, 1977), p. 76.

20. This use of *sobor* probably refers to the Kingdom of Heaven. The vision then points to a spiritual future after the end of the world.

21. Ibid., p. 76.

22. S. L. Frank, ed., *A Solovyov Anthology*, Natalie Duddington, trans. (New York: Charles Scribner's Sons, 1950), p. 11. Godmanhood was Soloviev's expression of the theodic future of the human who has experienced what Calvin called sanctification. Because the Greek fathers stressed the persons of the trinity more than the unknowable nature of God, the image of God in which a person was created was his or her own person or personality. Growth in the image of God, which Latin America's Dom Helder said was impossible due to poverty, to Soloviev meant becoming like God. He described this blessed state as Godmanhood, the goal of everyone's striving, although it was not clear that Soloviev included females in what seems a generic "man" in the English form of Godmanhood.

23. Ibid., p. 13.

24. James Billington, *The Icon and the Axe* (New York: Alfred Knopf, 1966), p. 468.

25. Bernice G. Rosenthal, *Dimitri Sergeevich Merezhkovsky and the Silver Age: The Development of a Revolutionary Mentality* (The Hague: Martinus Nijhoff, 1975), p. 168.

26. A loose paraphrase of Matthew 25:35–40.

27. Richard Shaull, "Revolutionary Change in Theological Perspective," in John Coleman Bennett, ed., *Christian Social Ethics in the Changing World: An Ecumenical Theological Enquiry* (New York: Associated Press, 1966), p. 33.

28. Jurgen Möltmann, *Religion, Revolution, and the Future*, M. Douglas Meeks, trans. (New York: Charles Scribner's Sons, 1969), p. 139.

29. Antonio Batista Fragoso, "Evangelo y justicia social," *Cuadernos de Marcha*, XVII, September 1968, 14.

30. Gustavo Gutierrez, *A Theology of Liberation: History, Politics, and Salvation*, Sister Caridad Inda and John Eagleson, trans. and eds. (Maryknoll, NY: Orbis Books, 1973), p. 35. Also see Thomas Sheehan, *The First Coming: How the Kingdom of God Became Christianity* (New York: Random House, 1986), pp. 61, 64.

31. Roger Johnson, in *Critical Issues in Modern Religion*, pp. 219–233.

32. Eduard Bernstein, *Evolutionary Socialism*, Edith C. Harvery, trans. (New York: B. W. Huebsch, 1912), pp. 142–144, cited in James R. Ozinga, *The Recurring Dream of Equality: Communal Sharing and Communism Throughout History* (Lanham, MD: University Press of America, 1996), pp. 208–209.

Chapter 6

Altruism and Absolute Goals

The third barrier to effective altruism lies in placing it in an absolute future. Altruism, and frequently all virtue, is then considered a part of the far off goals so absolute they become aspects of a perfect world. Virtuous activity, including altruism, becomes an activity for dreamers because the virtue is seen as part of perfection. Virtues like altruism are then noble concepts that one can imagine as real only in some past Golden Age or Garden of Eden, never to be seen again this side of heaven or some revolutionary future. Little things, like carrying something too heavy for someone else, or picking up a little boy's hat so that he won't lose it, or smiling at the lady who checks out the groceries, are denigrated. They are not considered to be altruism. If angels did not sing it is not altruism. So long as altruism is thought of as part of an absolute future it will forever seem unattainable because it has become such a perfect goal that it stifles action in the here and now. Altruist and saint are seen as synonymous. People cannot be altruistic because that would mean that they are perfect or almost perfect, whatever that would mean, and they would have to be perfect all the time. They could not feel anger when another driver pulled in front of them on the highway. It would mean behaving like that reprehensible teacher's pet we remember in the seventh grade.

This is all nonsense, of course. People in heaven would not have a choice about being good. Virtues like altruism only make sense where there is choice. So where does this absoluteness come from? The absoluteness comes from the sense of canonical orthodoxy in either religious or ideological thinking, which takes human characteristics of altruism, love, sense of fairness, and equality and turned them into ingredients of an impossible future. It is as though we were talking about needing a revitalized Golden Age or Garden of Eden experience in order to have altruism at all—an experience in some distant, very different future when we will be in heaven, or in a classless, propertyless communism, or even in a world without males.[1]

Virtue is not very well understood. Sometimes people think that only females can exhibit virtues such as sharing and caring, that only females really have these virtues. In males they would appear as effeminate, as unmanly. This idea may be a throwback to those very ancient days on Crete or in northern Africa when society was organized by women much more than by men.[2] If this is true, it explains the sense one develops that feelings of altruism and equality may make society more feminine. This idea may have begun in 1697 with Mary Ansell whose book, *A Serious Proposal to the Ladies for the Advancement of their True and Greatest Interest*, pushed the notion that society would be much more virtuous if women were educated and a part of it.[3] This idea was echoed seventy years later by Sarah Scott with her book about the residents of Millenium Hall.[4] Many of the themes found in paperback romance novels are visible here as basis to the serious message: the civilizing and humanizing influence of the female over the male, the beauty over the beast, innocence over the male wickedness, and so on. In addition to these two excellent books, there is a small body of science fiction literature that argues that a decent virtuous society is only possible if the men are first ejected.[5]

This idea is fun to discuss and may even have some common sense behind it, but perhaps the real reason altruism is so closely tied to utopian or 'absolute goals is that virtues saw the light of day first in the stories people heard about the ancient myths, in religious stories of creations and future heavens, and in the "secular" descriptions of a communist past and future penned by Karl Marx and Friedrich Engels. Note how absolute the notion of virtue is in the following.

Hesiod, for example. From the vantage point of the eighth century before Christ, Hesiod wrote in his poem *Works and Days* of the really ancient times when, he thought, it was obvious that men and gods had a common descent. In the beginning, he wrote, the immortals whose homes were on Olympus created the golden generation of mortal people. They lived in Kronus' time, when he was the king in heaven, living as if they were gods; hearts were free of all sorrow and there was no hard work or pain. No miserable old age came their way because their hands and feet did not alter. They took their pleasure in festivals, lived without troubles and, when they died, it was as if they had fallen asleep. All goods were theirs. The fruitful grainland yielded them a great and abundant harvest of its own accord while they at their pleasure quietly looked after their works in the midst of all the good things.[6] This was a heavenly past that gave people the feeling that we had something once, and we can get it again.

Ovid (43B.C.–17A.D.), a Roman poet, provides a later example of the same golden age myth. In Book I of his *Metamorphoses* he poetically described the golden past in a lengthy creation myth that comes just after Ovid has the Maker imbue formless, rude clay with human form. Contrary to the probably incorrect notion of a very short timespan in the Garden of Eden followed by a lot of hard work, Ovid suggested that early humans lived well over a lengthy period. When the world was very young and humans were rather new, Ovid felt that things were very nice. The Golden Age, he wrote, was lived without law or force. People did the right things without coercion. There wasn't any punishment nor even the fear of it. A person did not have to pray for mercy, there was no need. Everyone was secure and safe without walls or moats or horns or trumpets, and certainly there was safety without swords or shields. Nations could doze through the ages because they were safe without armies. The earth freely gave all that people needed without being worked by either spade or plowshare. Spring lasted throughout the year. Warm winds blew softly over the flowers that bloomed without seeds. Like the flowers the untilled earth brought forth profuse crops of grain from uncultivated fields. Life was easy and very pleasant in the Golden Age.[7]

According to Ovid, we lost the Golden Age. The rhythm of the pattern is that things go from gold to silver to brass and by the age of brass people know what cold and ice are and are learning the relation between work and survival. Then came the Age of Iron when, Ovid stated, modesty, truth, and faith withdrew, replaced by tricks, deceit, brute force, treachery, and a lust for gain. This is why virtues are thought of as part of the Golden Age but no other. Virtuous people were expected to stand out from society? Only rare individuals like Francis of Assisi or Mother Theresa could be virtuous? Strange and mistaken thinking.

Taoism, a Chinese religion and philosophy following the teachings of Lao-tse who lived in the Sixth century B.C., speaks of a time that used to be when people lived with birds and beasts and all creation was one. There was no good versus bad, for everyone was equally without knowledge and without evil desires; virtue could not err and everyone was in a state of natural integrity.[8]

Moreover, crime and violence are expected parts of society. People think that getting rid of such evils requires an absolute *bouliversment* in society, a throwing over of all of civilization's so-called progress and a return to a past, idyllic life. In one of his last plays, *The Tempest*, Shakespeare highlights these ideas in Gonzalo's speech in Act II, Scene 1 where the counsellor said that if he had the planting of this isle and were the king on it, he would not admit any sort of traffic, nor magistrate. Letters would be unknown on this evidently ignorant island. In the community there would not be any riches, nor poverty, nor service or contract or succession. No one would be bound to the land. There would be no use of metal, corn, wine, or oil. There would be no occupations because everyone would be idle, even the women, who would be innocent and pure. Of course there would be no sovereignty. Nature would produce all things in common without sweat or endeavor. There would thus be no need for crime of any sort, no need for weapons. Nature would bring forth a plentiful abundance that would feed my innocent people. Then, he continued, I would govern with such perfection as to surpass the Golden Age.[9] Virtue is tied here to innocence, to ignorance, to a primitive sort of equality; it is no wonder that so many people feel that altruism is a word that should be left to the golden future.

These ancient memories were reinforced by later stories in all the religions, such as the Judeo-Christian version of the beginnings in an idyllic Garden of Eden described in Genesis. This story, the creationists' alternative to human evolutionary beginnings, placed a first man and a first woman (Adam and Eve) in a garden probably located in the Middle East near Iran. There in the garden these two people lived in innocent happiness.

There was no mention of private property, illness, nighttime, or a host of other things ancient people felt were negative because this garden was supposed to be an absolute positive. Everything was good. Many of the items that were not mentioned may simply not yet have been thought of. Nonetheless, this beginning of human relations and human interactions with the environment was in a context of absolute good. If one had a picnic there would be no ants. No threat of a bee sting. There was an innocence in Eden that extended to plants and animals. No need to run from a fearsome beast; even fear was unknown until after the two people had eaten of the fruit from the forbidden tree.

They lived in harmonious peace with everything. Everything was theirs to use as needed, everything was held in common. Because the creation story appears to culminate in the creation of humans, it is natural to read this as grounds for human dominance of nature, but the focal point may well not have been that clearly formed in the beginning. All was in balance, one assumes, and that would mean that Adam and Eve had responsibilities toward the Garden as well as permission to take from the Garden. The two people were living in an earthly paradise. They had no desire for clothing and no sense that being naked was anything unusual. Additionally, there was no need to work for food, shelter, or happiness. Presumably, it was a warm climate because there was no suggestion that clothing was needed for warmth, and the earth provided for human hungers and needs apparently without any effort expended by Adam or Eve like the Golden Age; even though, unlike that Age, it was Adam's duty to dress and keep the Garden (Genesis 2:15). There was some activity that could be thought of as work, but it would be work that didn't seem like work to Adam. Nineteenth century socialists and communists often spoke like this, too. People would work in the future society, but work would be like doing a hobby. In Adam's case one gets the impression that it was easy work because all the animals were as irenic as the two people. Did Eve help with this work? Probably. There may not have been anything else to do before the children started coming.

They did not even know they were naked. There was no discomfort. This is still true of children. Even after children learn what nudity is they will still bathe unconcernedly with siblings of the other gender. They are innocents like Adam and Eve, or as kindergartners appear to be. And not only were they supposed to be innocents in the beginning, Jesus later taught that this was something people should become—like little children—or else entering the Kingdom of Heaven was said to be unlikely (Matt 18:3). The Kingdom was to be made up of people resembling little children (Luke 18:16). It seems strange that Eve (or Adam) should be blamed for trusting the serpent when trusting others is what an innocent child mostly does.

Just as with the Golden Age, or many later examples of communal sharing, the Garden of Eden experience was not as long lasting as one might have hoped, although Agostino Inveges (1649) speculated that the Garden of Eden experience began at dawn on Friday March 25 and ended at 4:00 p.m. on Friday April 1.[10] In Ovid's poem, the suggestion was made that the movement of the gods caused the Golden Age to slip into silver: Saturn was sent to gloomy hell and Jove ruled the world. Plato's *Republic* saw the overvaluing of honor as compared with wisdom as the culprit, and one moved from philosopher kings and queens to something he called a timocracy. The perfect society, in other words, develops a virus and begins to degenerate. Jean Jacques Rousseau's state of nature seemed very similar in that the perfections of the early beginning could not safeguard against emergent private property. Karl Marx, reflecting his Hegelian background, saw the virus or flaw as alienation that emerged in the "gens" society when people developed religion as a function of their alienation and allowed the notion of private property to evolve without serious challenge. As a result, both religion and private property were institutions that separated people from their own best character-istics and represented sin to the later Liberation Theologians. But as long as it lasted, Eden was absolutely good. To be virtuous meant to be in the Garden, vice was outside. The murder of Abel was unthinkable in the Garden, quite thinkable outside.

Similarly, the heaven in the sky. Absolute good plus eternal life and proximity to God, a state of absolute bliss enhanced by access to the tree of life. As in the beginning there is to be no sadness, hunger, difficulty, pain, or work. No tears, death, or sorrow (Rev 21:3-4).

In order to maintain the absolute goodness, however, one has to overlook some things. For example, the limited access of heaven suggests elitism. Another example is the very imperfect state of things just outside the walls. Rev 22:15 states that right outside the city were dogs, sorcerers, fornicators, murderers, idolaters, and liars. Clearly, heaven has nasty suburbs. The author of Revelations gives the reader the impression that heaven is a golden barge sailing on a very dirty Nile. Because most people do not read the book of Revelations, however, only the very positive things are remem-bered, even if vaguely.

The Jewish heaven is not that different, except that there seem to be many interpretations of it. Milton Steinberg wrote that there might be more varied descriptions of life after death among Jews than any other tenet of Judaism.[11] The form of the hereafter is called Paradise, Heaven, or Eden, and the opposite is called Hell, Sheol, or Gehinnom, the garbage dump outside of Jerusalem. At any rate, there is a deathlessness, a resurrection, a judgment day, a reward or punishment in the Jewish faith; and a heavy emphasis on the Kingdom and the need for the Messiah.[12] It would be perfect. Calves and young lions would play together and be led by a little child. There would be no hurting and no destroying in all God's holy mountain (Isaiah 65:25).

The Islamic heaven is expectedly similar in many respects because Islam is based on the Judeo–Christian tradition. However, in one interpretation of the Muslim heaven, that of the feast, the heaven appears to be more for men than women. In this view the heaven is a giant banquet with the men being served by young boys or pretty women.

In Buddhism and Hinduism life was seen as a dissatisfied existence searching for an otherworldly goal, rather like a moth being attracted by the impossible, such as the moon or a star. The cause of the dissatisfaction, or alienation, was attachment to things of sense, to things of the material world. Peace was not to be found in the acquisition of things, but in release through the limitation of desire. Nirvana, or release, was from individual consciousness to unity with all, an ending of rebirths and the bliss of connection with the deity.

Both Hinduism and Buddhism tend more toward abstract notions of heaven, but then they do not have much of a beginning story to match the Garden story of Christianity, Judaism, or Islam. Except for the possible gender distinctions in the Islamic heaven, there is in all religious belief a strong commitment to an egalitarianism that marks the end of distinctions between people. All are brothers and sisters, all that is that have made it to the promised future. Many do not, and for those unsuccessful ones there is an egalitarianism of despair in the place called hell or a continuation of life in another form.

Religions, therefore, began with altruism as a part of a lovely package of virtues: love, innocence, sharing, brotherhood or sisterhood, and equality as in the Garden of Eden. Those characteristics, however, were lost when alienation from God occurred. Overcoming that alienation permitted those seeking virtue to find earnests of that future Kingdom in this world and a full Kingdom of Heaven later. Secular descriptions of golden ages when life began are astonishingly similar to this religious story. Dreams of future worlds where people act altruistically and share in equality are similar as well whether one is looking at a religion or at a revolutionary ideology like Marxism.

An example of this similarity occurs in Dolores Ibarruri's autobiography, the story of her leading role in the evolution of Spanish communism. She had become a parliamentary deputy for the Spanish Popular Front in the 1936 elections and took her new job very seriously. When a man approached her office and said his pregnant wife, about to give birth, had been refused treatment in the maternity home because she could not pay, Dolores went back with him and demanded to see the manager. A nun went to get him and returned with him. The manager refused to readmit the woman even though her labor had begun. Dolores turned to the nun and said: "You're despicable!" "Where's your charity, your love of your neighbor?[13] Communism and Christianity had, for the Spanish communist Dolores Ibarruri, the same kind of virtue. It is most understandable.

In Marx's theories about the future, the secular goal was as absolute as was the religious one. Revolution, in this case the proletarian or worker revolution, would usher in a period called socialism to be followed after some time by a second and final period called communism. The chief difference between the period before the revolution and the one afterward is that a heavy dose of altruism and general virtue was added to the second period as the socialization of the means of production percolated upward through the society.

The Marxian explanation of this phenomenon was that a change in the means of production changed everything in society because the means of production were the dominant economic foundation of the society in any given epoch. Throughout history there were two major classes of society. They were the owners and the nonowners of the means of production. When change occured in the ownership of the means of production, the non-owners became the owners. In the last stages of property, when capitalism was in its death throes, the workers (proletariat) would seize the opportunity to throw off the yoke of the middle-class factory owners (bourgeoisie). If this proletarian revolution were a football game the contest would be between humanity on one side and the greedy capitalists on the other side: The time-honored struggle between virtue and vice.

Because the proletariat represented everyone, Marx felt, when they were successful it was the success of everyone, not simply the working class. So their victory did not mean a proletarianizing of the means of production, but a socializing of it, so that whereas before one class owned and the other class worked, one saw after the revolution the beauty of everyone owning and everyone working. Because the means of production no longer determined class the society was classless, and because history was a record of class warfare, of the rich against the poor, one now saw a situation where no hostility existed. Because the state was the oppressive arm of the ruling class, and there was no longer a ruling class, the state began to wither.

All of this is accomplished by the socialization of the means of production. In theory, the new society called socialism would be a society of brothers and sisters and love and sharing. A secular garden of eden or a secular heaven wherein altruism would flourish. But once again it is tied to a future on the other side of the socialization of the means of production.

The transition depended on that socialization, but what that meant in the real world no one knew, although many pretended. The Russian Bolsheviks interpreted this to mean that the ownership of the means of production was transferred from private to state ownership, but because Marx felt the state would quickly wither after the proletarian revolution and the dictatorship of the proletariat, it is quite likely that Marx would not have agreed with Lenin. If you do not transfer ownership to the state, but to something called the whole people, how does this get accomplished? Don't ask. It is as mysterious as how the soul gets to heaven when one dies.

The future was divided into two periods that revolved around the distribution of the social wealth. In socialism, the operative slogan would be "From each according to their ability, to each according to their work." How much a person worked would determine the size of his or her reward. Work eight hours and receive eight hours worth of goods. This was equality, Marx argued, that covered over the inequalities of strength, age, and the number of a person's dependents. When socialism had been internalized, after perhaps a generation or two, society would inscribe the familiar slogan on its banner: "From each according to their ability, to each according to their needs." Need would be the basic criterion, and reward according to need would finally divorce one's work from the share of social wealth received. Work would still be expected, but no longer because it was the means to satisfy animal needs. Work in late socialism and in communism would be performed as a means to satisfy one's human nature, one's desire to create, to produce.

Authority in the new society, whether socialism or communism, would emerge from an association that was fairly identical with the community. In his answer to Proudhon, a French anarchist, Marx wrote in *The Poverty of Philosophy* that the working class in the course of its development would substitute for the old civil society an association that excludes classes and class antagonism, and there would be no more political power because political power was precisely the official expression of class antagonism in civil society.[14]

Central authority without political power, redistribution of wealth without the power of the state, a worldwide society operating according to a single plan, somehow all coming together so as to sustain unbroken, progressive industrial development so that each would have an abundance, people wanting to work the fewer necessary hours, and the whole world at peace. Alienation would be over. Conflict no more, as peace spread throughout the world. This is as absolute as one can get. There is no imperfection in this theory as there are none in the Christian expectation.

Both religions and revolutionary ideologies required some kind of an apocalypse before the remembered kindness and sharing could be implemented. In both instances, the goal is a part of the absolute future rather than something anyone will seriously try in the present. Before that can happen, they are taught, there must be something magical called the socialization of the means of production, or we have to die in order to leave this world, or the end of the world has to come. The world as we know it is contaminated and we are inhibited from acting virtuously. Our absolute goals are a barrier to virtue.

There may be a way out of the perpetual problem if absolutes are left behind. The moment this is done, of course, there is the danger that nothing can be accomplished. Without the absolutist anchor one feels adrift, sensing that one has, unwisely, accepted half of a bridge as a compromise. So used to thinking of virtue as absolute it becomes less than virtuous when we compromise. Less than virtue has always meant vice or sin. Reacting in horror a person returns to the security of absolutes, no solution at all. One has to, heaven forbid, think these things out for oneself. For example, if one wants, like the nineteenth century socialist Etienne Cabet, to argue that some forms of private property are permissible in the sharing society, where does one draw the line? Too little equality and one has a sort of socialized capitalism, something conservatives in the United States argue we already have. Too much equality and the need for authoritarianism becomes very real.

Although it is not easy, if absolutes can be left behind one is in the position James Harrington (1611–1667) was in; trying to slip a different kind of utopia between More's regimented communist island ideas with too little liberty and Britain's veneration of private property for the few with far too little equality for the many. James Harrington's *Oceana* was a precedent for this kind of moderation. He tried to repair society rather than to restructure it completely. His ideal society was not "ideal." It was not absolute. It was more republican than communist, and his attitude toward property and property sharing indicated a sense of the importance of an equality goal that was a good distance from the absolute.

Harrington was part of the chaotic seventeenth century in Britain and a victim of the political see-saw that occurred. He had been an official of Charles I's court, and when the King was executed by parliamentary forces, Harrington retired to his estates at the age of thirty-seven, like others, pondering the future nature of the British political system. Thomas Hobbes published his analysis of what Britain needed in his book, *The Leviathan* in 1651. Hobbes argued for the restoration of a strong monarchy because he imagined that people lived in a dangerous anarchy prior to civil society. A strong sovereign was therefore needed to keep order and make civilization possible. Hobbes would have been more popular if he had argued that the sovereign's power came from God. But because Hobbes was an atheist he argued on different grounds and found himself isolated from other seventeenth-century royalists who justified the king's power by reference to a royal genealogy that went back to Adam and God. So Hobbes's ideas did not serve, but other intellectuals felt that their ideas might have a better reception.

The Commonwealth of Oceana was published both in answer to Hobbes and to express Harrington's ideas about the relation between property distribution and social stability. The novel was dedicated to the antiroyalist

Oliver Cromwell, the victor in the civil war, and was sufficiently successful that a group of influential people calling themselves "Harringtonians" petitioned Parliament in 1659 to consider establishing a commonwealth patterned after his utopia.

In 1661, Harrington wrote his *System of Politics* continuing the discussion of his ideas, but, despite his earlier popularity, the timing was ill-considered for any discussion of a commonwealth that did not need a king. The political system had shifted again and in 1660 the new king, Charles II, had been restored to the throne. Charles II did not care for Harrington's ideas. Harrington was arrested and imprisoned in 1661 and was harshly treated for several months before being released in ill health both physically and mentally. Although his ideas were moderate, he still got in deep trouble because his moderation was judged by an unfavorable absolutist, the king.

Harrington was not concerned about altruism but about property distribution, yet, his ideas make sense in any compromising ambience. His original contribution in *Oceana* was that the key to an analysis of any society was the distribution of property within that state. He wanted neither a narrow concentration of property in the hands of the few nor a too-wide decentralization of property in the hands of the many. Concentration in neither was desirable, but balance between them was. The nature of that balance determined whether the society was involved in civil war or was stable. Hobbes had argued that if one wanted stability one must choose a strong monarch whose force of arms would create the stability. Harrington argued that the choice between a strong king or a strong parliament was not the important one; the big question with reference to stability was the balance of property ownership, just as today the big question refers to how to reduce the size of the income gap. He wrote in *Oceana* that dominion was property, both real and personal property; lands, money, or goods. So, he argued, the nature of any empire can be determined by considering the proportion or balance of dominion or property in land. The proportion or balance of dominion or property in land determined the nature of the empire.[15]

Both Plato and Aristotle had argued that governments could be distinguished by the number of people involved (i.e., one, few, many), and by whether the rulers ruled in their own interest or in the interest of the society as a whole. Harrington's contribution was to describe a different understanding of what creates the nature of a political system: the distribution of property, both in lands and in goods. He argued that the real elements of power were riches, wealth, and property.[16] It was a more economic understanding of the political system. Concerned only with liberty, political systems can be described as republics or monarchies and not ever refer to the very important issue of property balance. Harrington pointed the way to change this method of political analysis over three centuries ago. In the language of the seventeenth century, he wrote that if one man were the sole landlord of a territory he had an absolute monarchy. If, however, a nobility plus a clergy were landlords, one has a mixed monarchy. But if the whole people were landlords, then one had a commonwealth.

The commonwealth was not based on the abolition of private property but rather on a sufficient redistribution of property so that many more possessed it. Altruism in this world, similarly, is not based on a destruction of selfishness but on an acceptance of selfishness as a legitimate and necessary part of the human character and an awareness of how altruism can ameliorate that selfishness in the human character. For example, Harrington argued that everyone being a landlord could mean everyone owning property, or it could mean that the property was so widely distributed that no one person or number of people could overbalance it.[17] If everyone, or almost everyone, tried to be altruistic much of the time, what a changed world this would be!

The balance of property ownership was correlated to the need of force in the society to achieve order, which was related to the balance between the political and economic system. The point made, contra Hobbes, was that force was an unreliable base of a society, that the more one depended on force the more unreliable was the form of government and the more unstable the political and economic system. Force was most necessary when the balance between property distribution and political power was skewed, as for example, the people having the most property, but with the political power in the hands of a single person, the king. The people in this example would not be dependent on the king for food, and would not need to serve the king so that the king would need to use his army to keep order. The royal army, in turn, would require vast supplies of goods and money, which would have to be wrested from the independent population through taxation. Not a stable structure, and civil war would probably ensue.[18] But in a republic when the number of property holders was increased, Harrington felt, there was a corresponding increase in the number of good soldiers, gentlemen, commoners or whatever.[19]

Public morality was also improved by increasing the number of property holders. Harrington's theory of balance argued that the source of all political power ought to be the ownership of property. That kind of balance made for stability. "Not having things makes men obedient; having things makes them independent."[20] This is why established interests do not want change, even moderate change. Established elites want people obedient, not independent, and that means maintaining large income gaps. This makes a great deal of sense.

In Harrington's *Oceana*, absolute equality (or liberty) would neither be expected nor desired. Harrington stood for a balance of property holding that would place private property in many more hands than in his own day, but private property would not be destroyed. In the past we have too often argued the need to eradicate the income gap as though the goal was to have no gap at all. Seeking the absolute creates so much opposition that the goal is entirely prevented. Similarly, people have sought altruism as though they each needed to become a St. Francis alongside the expressway, giving away all they had to those who passed. It is no wonder people rejected this idea as impractical. But the baby left with the bath water.

Keep in mind that the solution is a compromise, and that perhaps the methods need to be moderate as well. Over a century ago, a left Hegelian, Ludwig Feuerbach, wrote that he wanted people to find the determining factor of their lives in a loving that he saw as a body and soul actively living for others, for humanity, for universal ends. These words can get in the way of the solution because they demand a sacrifice that seems too heavy, but even more to the point they get in the way when it is forgotten, as Feuerbach himself pointed out, that these universal ends can only find actuality in concrete human form: "If I want equality, I want equal people, people with equal liberty,"[21] and I am then for whatever is necessary to enable people to possess an equal shot at life. If I want a more altruistic society, I need people (as well as myself) to seek the welfare of others as much as their own. In the language of liberation theology I must do the truth, engage in what can be called orthopraxis; activity designed to correct maladjustments or deformities, which is "far more important and far more consistent with the gospel than simply assenting to the truth (orthodoxy)."[22]

In the past, sick people were bled by barbers before the development of modern medicine. Some people may even have been helped by these strange methods. But not many. It is time the medicine for sick societies was also modernized. Instead of bleeding them through conflicts and hatreds and maintaining barriers to virtue, we can heal them. The Tree of Life is for the healing of nations. If this could happen people would find that the pathway to the "Kingdom" is an extremely satisfying goal by itself. We have obscured this for twenty-four centuries. When will the kingdom come, the disciples asked Jesus. It will not come by waiting for it, Jesus seems to have answered, because it is already here, spread out upon the earth. People just do not see it.[23]

The altruism path has been there all along. Absolute goals prevent us from reaching it and discourage us from walking it. All it takes is a beginning.

NOTES

1. Rosalind Miles, *The Women's History of the World* (New York: Harper and Row, 1988).

2. Ibid., pp. 3–17. See also Riane Eisler, *the Chalice and the Blade* (San Francisco, CA: Harper and Row, 1988).

3. Mary Ansell, *A Serious Proposal to the Ladies for the Advancement of their True and Greatest Interest* (London: Richard Wilkin at the

King's Head in St. Paul's Church-Yard, 1697).

4. Sarah Scott, *A Description of Millenium Hall and the Country Adjacent: Together with the Characters of the Inhabitants and such Historical Anecdotes and Reflections, as may excite in the reader Proper Sentiments of Humanity* (London: Printed for J. Newberry at the Bible and Sun, St. Paul's Churchyard, 1767).

5. See, for example, the 1915 book, Charlotte Perkins Gilman, *Herland* (New York: Pantheon Books, 1979); Mary E. Bradley Lane, "Mizora: A Prophecy," in Ruby Rohrlich and Elaine Hoffman Baruch, eds. *Women in Search of Utopia* (New York: Schocken, 1984); Sally Miller Gearhart, *The Wanderground: Stories of the Hill Women* (Boston, Alyson Publications, 1979); and Suzette Haden Elgin, *Native Tongue* (New York: Daw Books, 1984).

6. Doyne Dawson, *Cities of the Gods: Communist Utopias in Greek Thought* (New York: Oxford University Press, 1992), p. 13. For a slightly more difficult translation see Hesiod, *Works and Days*, lines 110–121, translated in Apostolos Athanassakis, *Hesiod: Theogony, Works and Days, Shield* (Baltimore: Johns Hopkins Press, 1983), p. 70.

7. Ovid, *Metamorphoses*, Book I, found in George Sandys, *Ovid's Metamorphosis; Englished, Mythologized and Represented in Figures*, K. Hulley and S. Vandersall, eds. (Lincoln: University of Nebraska Press, 1970). An easier to read, partial translation is by Robert M. Adams, ed. and trans. (New York: Norton, 1975), pp. 96–97.

8. Chuang Tzu, cited in Andrew Wilson, ed., *World Scripture: A Comparative Anthology of Sacred Texts* (New York: Paragon House, 1995), p. 224.

9. William Shakespeare, *The Tempest*, in William Aldis Wright, *The Complete Works of William Shakespeare* (Garden City, NY: Doubleday, 1936), p. 1308.

10. James G. Frazer, *Folklore in the Old Testament: Studies in Comparative Religion, Legend, and Law*, vol. 1 (London: Macmillan, 1919), pp. 183–184.

11. Milton Steinberg, *Basic Judaism* (New York: Harcourt Brace Jovanovich, 1975), p. 161.

12. Ibid., p. 165.

13. Dolores Ibarruri, *They Shall Not Pass: The Autobiography of La Pasionaria* (New York: International Publishers, 1966), p. 175.

14. Karl Marx, *The Poverty of Philosophy* (Moscow: Foreign Languages Publishing House, n.d.), p. 167.

15. James Harrington, *The Political Writings*, Charles Blitzer, ed. (New York: Liberal Arts Press, 1955), p. 44.

16. Michael Downs, *James Harrington* (Boston: Twayne Publishers, 1977), p. 18.

17. James Harrington, *Political Writings*, op. cit., pp. 44–45.

18. Michael Downs, *James Harrington*, p. 20.

19. Ibid., p. 26.

20. Ibid., p. 33.

21. Melvin Cherno, "Introduction to Ludwig Feuerbach," in Ludwig Feuerbach, *The Essence of Faith According to Luther*, Melvin Cherno, trans. (New York: Harper and Row, 1967), pp. 18–19.

22. Arthur McGovern, *Marxism: An American Christian Perspective* (Maryknoll, NY: Orbis Books, 1990), p. 178.

23. *Gospel of Thomas 113*, a serial collection of Jesus' sayings dating from about 50A.D., cited in John Dominic Crossan, *The Historical Jesus: The Life of a Mediterranean Jewish Peasant* (San Francisco, CA: Harper Collins, 1992), p. 229 and pp. 282–283.1

Part III

Invisible and Unexpected Altruism

The invisible altruism described in Part III refers to three very different behaviors. The first (Chapter Seven) describes an unacknowledged altruism that seems selfish but results in desirable goals. The behavior does not normally start out as altruistic but certainly can end that way. The second (Chapter Eight) describes an altruism that is usually called a practical tradition and highly valued. It can even be viewed nostalgically when looking back at it because it appears to be such an obvious case of group altruism. But this behavior can actually harm the participants, individually and socially because the altruism prevents economic progress. The third (Chapter Nine) behavior refers to an invisible altruism that expresses connections hitherto unacknowledged between humans and the world in which they live.

So the following three chapters deal with apparently simple but actually complex and difficult to grasp cases of social altruism not normally acknowledged as such: what Adam Smith called "trucking," what could be called agricultural retardation and economic stagnation in the name of tradition in both the older Africa and Russia, and, finally, an environmental altruism where the recipient of the altruistic activity is not a person, thing, or object, but all three and more at the same time.

Chapter 7

The Unexpected Altruism from Selfish Behavior

Altruistic cooperation can occur without reference to conscious intent on the part of the cooperator(s) when it is the unintended, public byproduct of doing something that is individually selfish. The issue can be addressed in three parts, through examples drawn from economics, sex, and politics. Each of these examples shows a selfish, indeed short-term gratification sought for the private individual that is, nonetheless, locked symbiotically with a long-term, public, cooperative gain.

The first case comes from economics and is the longest, in part because it is the prevailing view that "[a]ltruism and nonprofit entrepreneurship cannot be understood within the standard economic framework.[1] This is odd because the primary example of this sort of altruism is drawn from a well known and respected source: the reference made by Adam Smith to the "invisible hand" in Book 4 of Chapter II of *Wealth of Nations*. He wrote that the individual does not intend to promote the general interest nor does she know by how much she is promoting it. He or she prefers to support the domestic rather than foreign industry so as to provide his or her own security. Indeed, by directing an industry in such a manner so as to produce products of the highest value, intending only personal gain, a person is led by an invisible hand to promote an end that was no part of his intention. Nor is society badly off from this serendipitous activity on its behalf. Smith wrote that by pursuing that personal interest the interests of the society would be promoted more effectively than if the person had consciously tried to promote social interests rather than his or her own.[2]

So, the first example is one of the private pursuit of economic gain locked into a relationship of mutual dependence with the increase in public wealth; not by intention or design, but by virtue of the symbiosis between private and public wealth. The resulting philosophy was called laissez-faire and meant either minimal or entirely no governmental interference in business and economics.[3] In general, the symbiosis was never understood, and the economic philosophy generally attributed to Smith was that letting people seek their selfish economic goals was the best thing for society as a whole. Instead of seeing how selfish behavior was locked into social altruism, the selfishness was itself underscored as a virtue, which in turn lead to economic modeling based on self-interest and "rational choice" or "public choice" modeling, which also assumed self-interest as the sole motivation. Even so, Anthony Downs wrote, in reality people were not always selfish, even in politics. They frequently did what appeared to be individually irrational because they believed it was socially rational (i.e., it benefited others even though it harmed them personally).

> For example, politicians in the real world some-
> times act as they think best for society as a
> whole even when they know their actions will
> lose votes. In every field, no account of human
> behaviour is complete without mention of such
> altruism; its possessors are among the heroes
> [others] rightly admire. Nevertheless, general
> theories of social action always rely heavily on
> the self-interest axiom.[4]

But even this awareness of the need for altruism misunderstood Smith. The social context of the ubiquitous trucking was not to be left to chance. The emphasis Smith placed on the context reaches an awareness, already in the eighteenth century, of how the social context affects behavior. According to Jane Mansbridge, this is a relatively new discovery. In the last ten years, she wrote, biologists have shown that social contexts affect human and animal biology. Menstruation in one woman can alter menstrual patterns in another. Eliminating a higher ranking vervet monkey in a dominance hierarchy can cause a rise of serotonin in the second ranked monkey. As evidence mounts that even the biological self is socially constituted, the very concept of self-interest becomes more complex.[5]

A rediscovery of the importance of the social context of self-interest might not have had to have been made in public choice theory if Adam Smith had been understood from the beginning. Laissez-faire was an argument against mercantilism, and was not by itself intended as a philosophy of life.

Smith's main point was that everyone pursuing his or her own economic interests promoted the public good and that therefore a free market was best. What was and is not understood is that the social good, the wealth of the nation in economic terms, does not derive from the unfettered economic activity of a few, but of all economic actors.

Adam Smith was a moral philosopher, not a right-wing economist arguing against any form of social or government controls on the free market.

It sometimes seems to me that Adam Smith, that gentle soul from Kirkauldy, was confused with Bernard Mandeville who wrote his *Fable of the Bees* earlier in the eighteenth century. Mandeville argued that society was based neither on friendly or kindly qualities of human nature nor on virtue acquired by reason and self-denial, but rather on what we call evil in the world, moral as well as natural. Evil, he argued, is the grand principle that makes us sociable creatures, the solid basis, the life and support of all trades and employments without exception. Rich and poor alike would not work unless driven to it by hunger. He was against any form of welfare to protect the poor, against any kind of education for the lower classes. Mandeville argued that the wealth of a nation consisted of a multitude of laborious poor kept as ignorant as possible.

Knowledge both enlarges and multiplies our desires, Mandeville wrote, and the fewer things a person wishes for, the more easily the necessities may be supplied.

> Going to school in comparison to working is idleness, and the longer boys continue in this easy sort of life, the more unfit they'll be when grown up for downright labour, both as to strength and inclination. Men who are to remain and end their days in a laborious, tiresome, and painful station of life, the sooner they are put upon it at first, the more patiently they'll submit to it for ever after.[6]

The reason for introducing Mandeville is to demonstrate that this kind of thinking about the social context is definitely not Adam Smith. Smith was not arguing for a market freedom that was really market anarchy with people at the mercy of uncontrollable forces. He was not advocating a moral economy without moral purpose. Much to the contrary, he advocated a market system in which the whole purpose was consumption. These ideas were very clearly put forth in his 1759 publication *The Theory of Moral Sentiments* which went through four editions before *Wealth of Nations* came out in 1776, and a fifth edition after *Wealth* came out. *Moral Sentiments* was translated into French three times. The last edition, the one after *Wealth*, was revised by Smith and he added a last chapter with this long title: "Of the Corruption of Our Moral Sentiments, which is Occasioned by the Disposition to Admire the Rich and the Great, and to Despise or Neglect Persons of Poor and Mean Condition." Far from being the guru of reactionary economists, or of public choice theorists who see only rational, selfish individual actors articulating their interests in a social void, Smith argued for the importance of sympathy among the private producers. He stated in *Sentiments* that there were many occasions when the interests of the individual had to make way for the interests of others—regardless of any calculations of private utility. One individual, he wrote, must never prefer himself so much even to any other individual as to hurt or injure that other, in order to benefit himself, even though the benefit to the one should be much greater than the hurt or injury to the other. Think of all the self-serving praise for capitalism that implies that one must simply get used to stepping on others in order to get ahead. That's the way the game is played. Not, however, according to Adam Smith.

> The wise and virtuous man is at all times willing
> that his own private interest should be sacrificed
> to the public interest of his own particular order
> of society. He is at all times willing, too, that
> the interest of this order or society should be
> sacrificed to the greater interest of the state or
> sovereignty, of which it is only a subordinate
> part. He should, therefore, be equally willing
> that all those inferior interests should be sacri-
> ficed to the greater interest of the universe.[7]

Moral Sentiments and *Wealth of Nations* were two parts of a grand design. He had *Wealth* in mind when he wrote *Sentiments* and *Sentiments* in mind when he wrote *Wealth*. His political economy was part of his larger moral philosophy. His own words provide the evidence.

> Our merchants and master-manufacturers com-
> plain much of the bad effects of high wages in
> raising the price, and thereby lessening the sale
> of their goods both at home and abroad. They
> say nothing concerning the bad effects of high
> profits. They are silent with regard to the
> pernicious effects of their own gains. They
> complain only of those of other people.[8]

The loud sophistry of merchants and manufacturers, Smith wrote, easily persuades them that the private interest of a part, and of a subordinate part of the society, is the general interest of the whole. "People of the same trade seldom meet together, even for merriment and diversion, but the conversation ends in a conspiracy against the public, or in some contrivance to raise prices."[9]

Moreover, the proposal of any new law or regulation of commerce that comes from this order of manufacturers and merchants, ought always to be listened to with great precaution, and ought never to be adopted till after having been long and carefully examined, not only with the most scrupulous, but with the most suspicious attention. "It comes from an order of men, whose interest is never exactly the same with that of the public, who have generally an interest to deceive and even to oppress the public, and who accordingly have, upon many occasions, both deceived and oppressed it."[10]

"It is the industry which is carried on for the benefit of the rich and powerful, that is principally encouraged by our mercantile system. That which is carried on for the benefit of the poor and the indigent, is too often, either neglected, or oppressed."[11] Little did Smith realize that his own words would be twisted to support the same idea long after mercantilism had been uprooted.

Self-interest was itself a moral principle to Smith—a principle fundamentally conditioned by a restraining social context. Although the baker does not create edibles because of benevolence, but out of self-interest, nonetheless this self-interest was predicated on the assumption that the baker would not take advantage of others, but would abide by the rules of the free market, and not conspire to deceive or oppress.

And, when discussing the wealth of the nation, Smith argued that the well-being of the poor was an important part of that wealth. What improves the lot of this greater part of society improves the whole and was not an inconvenience. It is only fair, he wrote, that the poor have such a share of the produce of their labor so as to permit themselves to be tolerably well fed and clothed.[12] Nor was this concern for the poor an afterthought—his attacks on mercantilism were partly motivated by his concern for the poor. His notion of a free market, a "natural" system wherein people were left alone, would chiefly benefit the poor, he thought, not the rich; not giving the poor a handout to be wasted, but the opportunity to improve.

The liberal reward of labor, to use his own words, as it encourages the propagation so it increases the industry of the common people. The wages of labor are the encouragement of industry, which like every other human quality, improves in proportion to the encouragement it receives. A plentiful subsistence increases the bodily strength of the laborer, and the comfortable hope of bettering one's condition, and of ending one's days perhaps in ease and plenty, animates the worker to exert that strength to the utmost.

> Where wages are high, accordingly, we shall
> always find the work[people] more active, dili-
> gent, and expeditious, than where they are low:
> in England, for example, than in Scotland; in the
> neighbourhood of great towns, than in remote
> country places.[13]

Smith's optimism was more democratic, more mass oriented than that of the *philosophs* who distrusted the masses and wanted reforms to come from the top down. The transforming negative of the alienative force of the assembly lines he advocated would be matched, he hoped, by the positively transforming character of education. The common people would be taught reading, writing, and arithmetic in state-supported schools. Fees charged would be very modest and within people's ability to pay. To make it more "compulsory" Smith felt that before anyone could enter a guild or take up a trade, they should pass an exam in the three Rs. This was a revolutionary idea in the eighteenth century, because the dominant view was Mandeville's position: the more ignorant you kept the masses of people, the more content they would have to be with their lot.

Was this laissez-faire? Partially. Smith argued for laws that limited bankers' rights to issue notes, for laws against usury, and for support of the Poor Laws which had been in place since Elizabeth I. He argued for progressive taxation tied to ability to pay, and for taxes on luxuries rather than on necessities. He protested against laws that allowed masters to combine but not workers, over a century ahead of his time. The old mercantile system depended in principle on a system of regulations derived from equity, tradition, and law; a system prescribing fair prices, just wages, customary rights, corporative rules, paternalistic obligations, hierarchical relationships—all of which were intended to produce a structured, harmonious, stable, secure, and organic order. His system was one of natural liberty, priding itself on being open, mobile, changeable, individualistic, and possessing risks but also opportunities. Adam Smith's ideas, contrary to the state-involved economy, were seriously meant, carefully thought-out prescriptions for a sick society. He hoped his ideas would achieve

> a liberating, expanding, prospering, progressive
> economy in which the legitimate values and
> interests of society supported and reinforced each
> other; liberty and prosperity, the individual and
> society, industry and agriculture, capital and
> labour, wealth and well-being.[14]

But the point is that the political economy was a means to an end, not an end itself. The end was the wealth and well-being of the people, of whom the laboring classes were the largest part. Just as *Wealth of Nations* alone without *Moral Sentiments* does not adequately portray Adam Smith's position, so also a description of the social actor as a rational, individual self-sufficer is insufficient because it leaves out empathy as well as the social context in which the action occurs. If empathy is left out of the equation, the contract is one that Hobbes would recognize: I make a contract with you wholly in my favor.

Christopher Jencks argued the importance of this vicarious feeling of empathy, but he located the source of the empathy in government or society at large rather than with the individual. He wrote as though, if the society did not provide this, we would not have it.:

> the viability of the social contract depends not just on society's capacity to inspire fear in the hearts of potential violators, but on its capacity to develop the empathic tendencies from which moral sentiments derive. If a society can do this, it can expect its members to act unselfishly at least some of the time.[15]

Jencks was still mentally mired in the quicksand of the rational self-satisfier. Smith's whole point was that if people were left alone and rewarded justly, they would act both in their own and others' interests. His invisible hand was a metaphor for the innate empathy people possess that results in unconscious cooperation.

Gerard deZeeuw of the University of Amsterdam wrote that increases in the governability of social systems may increase individual competence, but decrease collective competence. When this increase in governability comes from above, or as deZeeuw said, when the conditions for competent implementation of activities are fixed by some super-actor, or by a stronger actor, a decrease in both individual and collective competence occurs.[16] Like the adult children helped too much by doting parents, people are being taught to be dependent. Another example to illustrate this point is the imposition of the command economy in the Soviet Union. Originally a means to the end of constructing the wealth of capitalism that Marx had assumed for the sharing in communism, the command economy became an end in itself, an ideology that replaced Marxism–Leninism,[17] and in the process reduced the competence of the system both individually and collectively.

Clearly, if one wishes to increase cooperation among people one needs to be careful about the kinds and scope of social institutions imagined to focus properly the cooperative spirit. The increased governability of systems can become such a negative example because, as deZeeuw pointed out, collective competence can actually diminish as a result. Obviously, this is important only if competence not governability is the end.

To come at this point from another direction, public choice theory demonstrates the inutility of first of all assuming a rational selfish actor in the economic sphere and then extending that rational selfishness into the political and other spheres. Steven Kelman, writing in 1987, was very critical of public choice theories and of the assumption of rational selfishness at the core of economic humanity. In this I agree. But Kelman erred when he assumed that self-interested maximization theories began with Adam Smith.[18] It is not only that public choice theory is far too narrow to be valuable, it is that the narrow economic theory that imagines itself based on Adam Smith deliberately discards the unconscious altruism that Smith went to such great lengths to describe. The ingrained tendency to truck and barter and the basic sympathy or empathy with which the individual begins can find a happy home in capitalism only if the people are left alone and government provides protection to ensure equivalency for the trucking.

Unconscious altruism is not limited to economics, nor to the peculiarities of Scottish moralists as my second example, sex and parenting, reveal.

Sexual relations between a woman and a man are primarily motivated by sexual desire, which seeks a selfish excitement and release because experience teaches that it is incredibly pleasurable. This activity usually becomes distorted by perverse mental hang-ups, but the main goal is the individual receiving and (ideally) giving of pleasure. The symbiotic macro-cosm with which the micro act of sex is related is the perpetuation of life. This is not accidental; the peak of a woman's libido is also the high point of her fertility. Moreover, there is more cooperation built-in to this macrogoal than one might think. The extension of life cannot operate without a social context that stimulates sympathetic co-operation. The social role with which the macrocosmic goal is achieved is called parenting. Our sexual pleasure seeker is confronted with children, often formed unknowingly, who demand a prolonged and costly altruism that was no part of the original "trucking."

Professor Virginia Held, a professor of philosophy at the City University of New York, has argued persuasively that the parent–child relationship, the social context of life extension, exhibits a number of characteristics that clearly mark this important and ubiquitous relationship off from incorrectly understood economic relations thought to be universally descriptive.[19] The parent–child relation is very different from the selfish behavior that caused it. Contrary to the ideas of Harvard's John Rawls, it is very different from the contracting relationship, which Rawls uses as the facilitator of natural duty and as a basis for a concept of moral equality between people.[20]

Why? Because parent–child relationships are so seldom voluntary, certainly not for the children and often not for the parent either. Second, because the parent–child relationship is largely permanent and non-replaceable. Third, the parent–child relation demonstrates that responsibilities are not fulfilled by leaving the person alone. Infants and children are dependent and the relationship provides insights into how equality might be shaped in the larger society. And the notion of equality that emerges is less about equal rights and more about equal consideration of other persons. Our notion of power is also affected. Power is not domination, but a prolonged effort to empower through transformative growth in the child. And fourth, the parent child relationship underscores the value of privacy. Being in a position where people are not making demands on us is a rare luxury whether this insight applies to the parent or the child.

Thus, the unintended consequence of private sexual pleasure, similar to our previous discussion in the economic sphere, is unconscious cooperation to achieve macro ends. This pattern seems clear as well when one looks at the polis, the third example of unconscious altruism.

We take organized societies for granted, but if political systems are assessed there is a lesson there also about unconscious cooperation in symbiotic relation to private pleasure. Organized societies are made possible by people doing different things. Those people are doing those different things for a variety of reasons, and almost all of those reasons are short-term, individual gratification. But that isn't the whole story. The motivation for all that activity is more than financial reward. People, to quote Marx's *Economic and Philosophic Manuscripts*, do not just work to live, they also live to work because working, creating, and producing is an intrinsic part of being a human. Aristotle said this better than Marx when he argued that the motivation for all behavior was happiness, but this happiness could not be pursued directly—it was the significant byproduct of performing at fever pitch what one did best. Therein lay virtue as well. But what did an individual need in order to exercise that virtue, to perform what one does best at fever pitch? The individual needed the polis, the organized society that was large enough to admit of sufficient specialization that a place is created for the individual's own contribution. Aristotle could not imagine one without the other—it was a symbiosis so vital that he insisted the state be logically prior to the individual.

Moreover, the microlevel and the macrolevel in this example are both as characterized by the need for empathy and cooperation as our earlier two examples. On the microlevel we need people unlike ourselves, different from ourselves, in order for our systems to function. Moreover, our relationship with those unlike ourselves has to be in the context of a real toleration of ambiguity, not an uneasy bargain whereby each constantly tries to bend the other his or her way or puts up only reluctantly with the intervals when the other prevails. Toleration of ambiguity means acceptance of difference without trying to erase it or render it insignificant with derogatory names. Relationships on the macrolevel involve real outgoing sympathy, which is to say, the accepting of ends that are not, at one time, one's own ends at all, Midgley continued, although acceptance may make them so.

> This is not inconsistent with *being oneself*, since oneself is not really designed as an exclusive system. But it is inconsistent with drawing a rigid line round those like one as the only beings with whom one should associate. A rational being is someone who sees himself as a unit among others, not as the core of the universe.[21]

On the macroperspective, cooperation in the polis is what makes the system work. Look at your favorite city sometime and see the cooperation at work. Buses, trucks, cars, taxis, trams, pedestrians, delivery services, elevators, flush toilets, electricity, water, natural gas, sewers, street sweepers, gas stations, pigeons, herring or hot dogs at the corner stand—unintended 'cooperation operating within the city that creates the possibility of virtue for the individual who pursues virtue, doing of what one does best for basically selfish reasons.

The individual cannot find happiness or virtue outside the political system, so here also the selfish activity of the individual is in symbiosis with a larger, cooperative social context called a political system. Individuals work at what pleases them, and society benefits, but society is also indispensable to the individual worker just as the wealth of the nation was indispensable to the individual who was trucking and bartering and just as parenting was indispensable to sex.

Unexpected macrocooperation in symbiotic relation to private, selfish activity.

NOTES

1.   Susan Rose-Ackerman, "Altruism, Nonprofits, and Economic Theory," *Journal of Economic Literature*, vol. 34, June 1996, p. 701.

2.   Adam Smith, *An Inquiry into the Nature and Causes of the Wealth of Nations* (Chicago: University of Chicago Press, 1976), p. 477.

3.   The minimal interference definition comes from an economics text. The definition reads: a program of minimal interference with the workings of the market system—people should be left alone in carrying out their economic affairs;   William J. Baumol and Alan S. Blinder, *Economics: Principles and Policy*, Second Edition (New York: Harcourt Brace Jovanovich, 1982), p. 433.   The noninterference definition comes from *Webster's New Universal Unabridged Dictionary*, Deluxe Second Edition (New York: New World Dictionaries/Simon and Schuster, 1979), p. 1015.

4.   Anthony Downs, *An Economic Theory of Democracy* (New York: Harper and Row, 1989), p. 29.

5.   Jane Mansbridge, "The Rise and Fall of Self-Interest in the Explanation of Political Life," *Beyond Self-Interest*, Jane Mansbridge, ed. (Chicago: University of Chicago Press, 1990), p. 18.   For more details on the social nature of menstruation, see Natalie Angier, "Study Finds Signs of Elusive Pheromones in Humans," *The New York Times*, March 12, 1998, p.18.

6.   Bernard Mandeville, *The Fable of the Bees*, Philip Harth, ed. (London: Printed at a variety of locations from 1714 into the 1730s.   The 1733 edition, for example, was printed for J. Tonson at Shakespeare's-Head over against Katherine-Street in the Strand), pp. 294–295.   This well known book was cited by Gertrude Himmelfarb, *The Idea of Poverty: England in the*

Early Industrial Age (New York: Alfred A. Knopf, 1984), p. 30.

7. Adam Smith, *A Theory of Moral Sentiments* (London: Richardson, 1822), cited in Himmelfarb, p. 48.

8. Adam Smith, *An Inquiry into the Nature and Causes of the Wealth of Nations* (Chicago: University of Chicago Press, 1976) pp. 98, 128, 250, 609; cited in Himmelfarb, p. 48.

9. Ibid.

10. Ibid.

11. Ibid.

12. Ibid., pp. 78–79; Himmelfarb, p. 51.

13. Adam Smith, *Wealth of Nations*, p. 81; Himmelfarb, p. 52.

14. Himmelfarb, p. 53.

15. Christopher Jencks, "Varieties of Altruism," in Jane Mansbridge, ed., *Beyond Self-Interest*, p. 59.

16. Gerard deZeeuw, "Social change and the design of enquiry," in Felix Geyer and Johannes van der Zouwen, eds., *Sociocybernetic paradoxes: Observation, Control and Evolution of Self-steering Systems* (London: Sage, 1986), pp. 143–143.

17. James R. Ozinga, "The End of Ideology in the Soviet Union," in Michael Urban, ed., *Ideology and System Change in the USSR and Eastern Europe* (London: MacMillan, 1991).

18. Steven Kelman, "Public Choice and the Public Spirit," *The Public Interest*, Spring 1987, p. 81.

19. Virginia Held, "Mothering versus Contract," in Jane Mansbridge, ed., *Beyond Self-Interest*, pp. 297–301.

20. J. Rawls, *A Theory of Justice* (London: Oxford University Press, 1971), p. 19, cited in Will Kymlicka, *Contemporary Political Philosophy* (Oxford: Clarendon Press, 1990), p. 126.

21. Mary Midgley, *Beast and Man: The Roots of Human Nature* (Ithaca, NY: Cornell University Press, 1978 [Meridian paperback edition published by The New American Library in New York]), 356–357.

Chapter 8

Harmful Altruism: Rural Equality in Africa and Russia

Altruism is not always beneficial to the recipient. It can be caught up in tradition and have damaging results over time when it seeks to perpetuate an unnatural egalitarianism, seeks to preserve an equality that should be allowed to dissolve naturally. Too much equality is not natural and harm results from its prolongation. Two clear examples of this are African extended family networks and the Russian serf system, both of which sought to perpetuate and preserve rural equality long past its time. Putting it very simply, this "harmful altruism" prevented modernization in those societies.

Modernization refers to historical events that focus on the dual process of improving and modifying traditional political institutions for the purpose of achieving industrialization or economic development. Normally, when one thinks of this subject one has in mind an Anglocentric frame of reference in that the modernization is expected to occur throughout the world pretty much as it developed in Britain.

This Anglocentric frame of reference is nonetheless faulty because modernization in other areas was (is) not similar. For example, modernization has in most cases not led to democracy because the preconditions for political democracy mentioned by de Tocqueville were never met; preconditions such as the repudiation of the feudal past, the triumph of the nonprivileged over the aristocrats, and the victory of the Third Estate.[1]

In this non-Anglocentric ambience, the industrial revolution or industrial capitalism found little or no soil in which to take root. Why? One answer suggested is that in those areas so different from the Anglocentric model, the necessary rural social differentiations were (are) retarded because an enforced egalitarianism haunted (s) the subsistence agricultural scene. Whether in the African extended family networks or in Russian serfdom, persistent harmful altruism created a premodernization egalitarianism that interfered with the painfully slow process of rural differentiation, preventing economic progress or fundamentally detouring it in the direction of a bifurcated society.

The lack of rural social differentiation meant that the division of successful from unsuccessful farmers, the precursor to capitalized agriculture, never took place. Without capitalized agriculture the English Industrial Revolution could not have occurred; no proletariat, no surplus food for cities or export, and an absence of the risk-taking that underlies capitalism.

This lack of differentiation in different contexts has been noticed by others; a class visible well beyond its historical period or classes anticipated but barely visible. Johan Huizinga wrote that the life form of the nobility in the Middle Ages retained its relevance over society long after the nobility as a social structure had lost its dominant meaning.[2] Conversely, he wrote, the French bourgeoisie were "underestimated," because "in the concept of the third estate, the bourgeoisie and the workers remained undifferentiated up until the time of the French Revolution."[3] This failure to estimate and therefore to differentiate resulted in an underutilization of the bourgeoisie in those countries with insufficient stratification.

This had astonishing consequences in the thinking of a revolutionary like Karl Marx. The evident failure of the Germans to revolt in 1848 was laid to the failure of the bourgeoisie to carry out their revolutions, and "since the bourgeoisie had proved incapable of making their own revolution, the working class would have to rely exclusively on its own forces."[4] In 1917 sentiments such as these led to the Bolshevik seizure of power in Russia and a sharing of poverty rather than wealth.

Other examples of too rapid or too slow a development come to mind. For instance, constitutional government is seen as an empirically superior manifestation of historical evolution, a bias affecting Western attitudes toward the traditions and aspirations of the non-Western majority of the world's population. David Hume, an eighteenth-century philosopher of note, wrote that the three fundamental laws of human nature, that is, laws present in humans everywhere in the eighteenth century, were those of stability of possession, of its transference by consent, and of the performance of promises.[5] He implied that a sense of property, made so much of by John Locke in 1691, four decades before, was universal when he should have known better, even in 1737 when he wrote those words. F. W. Watkins, writing on Hume, observed in 1953 that the bias regarding constitutional government was still visible 216 years later. Under the influence of scientific empiricism, Watkins wrote, liberal theorists tended toward mildly conservative utilitarianism. Rejecting *a priori* standards of political morality, they defend the institutions and practices of constitutional government as empirically superior manifestations of an historical evolution. As a result, Watkins continued, an

aristocratic and conservative bias quite similar to
that of Hume has normally been characteristic of
the Western liberal attitude toward the traditions
and aspirations of the non-Western majority of
mankind.[6]

This explanation accounts for the sense of superiority Anglocentric
observers have, but it does not explain why differences arose. All differences
are not to be explained here, but a major one can be the reason the industrial
revolution was unable to penetrate much of Africa and Russia in the nineteenth
and early twentieth centuries. Traditional egalitarianism in the subsistence
agriculture of these areas inhibited the rural differentiation so visible in the
Anglocentric model. Misplaced altruism in the African and Russian agricultural systems explains why these areas have progressed so little, and why
modernization has been so very difficult and different from the Anglocentric
expectations.

It isn't the altruism that is the problem, it's the timing. For example,
on Lady Musgrove Island off east Australia, at the southern end of the Great
Barrier Reef, the white-topped, black nodding tern occasionally will do a
stupid thing. Having mated for life, the tern left sitting on the eggs in the nest
will sometimes miss the spouse and simply get up and leave the nest to go find
the better half. This, unfortunately, leaves the eggs vulnerable to other birds'
attacks, and although the searching action may be called altruistic, it is an
altruistic behavior that endangers the germ line and must therefore be called a
potentially harmful altruism.[7] At other times, when the eggs have hatched and
the young are coping on their own, the act of altruism, seeking one's missing
mate, is in synchronization with the rest of the scene. Other instances of this
misguided and potentially dangerous altruism might be found, if one looked.
The defining characteristic is that the action meant as altruistic and even
normally considered altruistic results in harm to both the society and the
individual.

But in both the African and the Russian historical worlds, the areas
lay outside the scope of the industrial revolution into the modern era. This
was taken as backwardness, and as a "not yet" condition awaiting more
Western assistence and more indigenous learning. The industrial revolution
was not seen as a revolution blocked out of a society because of too much
egalitarianism in the rural areas, it was seen as something that yet awaits the
supposedly backward society. Professor Lucy Mair, for example, wrote in
1974 that social anthropologists study those parts of the world that have not
yet experienced the full consequences of the industrial revolution—where
people still get a large part of their living from the food they grow themselves
and the animals they herd, in which most of them expect the place they were

born to be their permanent home. The people "rely for cooperation on their kin and neighbours and not on contracts to do jobs for a money wage."[8] We must take as our starting point in studying these societies, she wrote, the fact that

> the peoples we are dealing with have not had,
> until they were brought to them from outside,
> the techniques of production and communication
> that the industrial world is used to. They belong
> to what Peter Laslett has called 'the world we
> have lost....'[9]

Or, E. Wayne Nafziger, writing in 1995, said much the same thing when he wrote that "modernization theorists have emphasized capitalist Japan as an alternative model to the socialist approach." From 1638 to the 1860s, he wrote, the Tokugawa shogun provided a more favorable ambience for industrialization than many of the sub-Saharan African countries. Mid-nineteenth century Japan, he wrote, had a literacy rate nearly as high as England, a good, integrated transport system, a well-developed tax system, and a highly commercialized agriculture.[10]

People see the problem but they do not know what they see. These areas were not so much behind as different. Both the African and Russian systems in the past had very different backgrounds from the Anglocentric model. In African systems the failure to differentiate was caused by very strong patterns of kinship obligations. Societies like the Maori in far off New Zealand were similar. Among the Maori the kinship affiliations of people deeply influenced their position in economic affairs. Kinship normally coincided with the local group and this dramatically affected work associations, the holding of land, and the use of its products.[11]

In a society like the Maori, no relationship was purely economic in character. Economics was within a social framework and the life of the community was regulated by a number of powerful forces combining and interacting with personal temperament and characteristics to shape the conduct of each individual.[12] The result? No extreme poverty, no unemployed wanting work in order to live, no leisure class in blissful idleness. This sounds like More's *Utopia*, and was in fact considered a communal ideal based on claims of kinship permitting an absence of a money economy and even direct material rewards for effort. Professor Firth wrote that "the attention of the native to the standards set him by tradition and communal opinion sufficed to secure the performance of duties otherwise neglected."[13] In Russia, on the other hand, the progressive enserfment of the peasantry caused the problematic situation.

Professor Mair wrote of African societies that the most significant relationship of these societies was (is) kinship. "Indeed our subject has been described as the study of kinship *par excellence*...."[14] In kinship systems, she wrote, in most African societies, people trace their descent unilineally, that is through father to father's father, or mother to mother's mother, as far back as they can go.

> Persons linked by either mode of descent form lineages, which are the source of rights to inheritance and are sometimes held collectively responsible for debts incurred or offences committed by any of their members; in societies which allow private revenge it is lineage mates who have the right and duty of avenging the death of one of their number.[15]

In a society such as this, the tribe, family, and social organization are the same and are much more important than the individual. The welfare of the community is of greater concern than that of the individual because survival may depend on it.[16] Assuming that economic progress is desirable, it is stifled by what had previously worked for survival. Approaches aimed at improving African agriculture by the introduction of large-scale modern schemes using directed labor have had little success.[17] The result: a labor intensive agricultural economy, unable to support an industrial revolution.

Tribalism had its positive side, of course. It provided economic sustenance through the sharing of incomes and a sense of identity for the poor and the uneducated. But it extended too far into the modern era and stifled economic development. So when the pressures of nation building were felt, democracy was only a gleam in the eye of a dreamer.

Moreover, the harmful altruism is involuntary. It is demanded by tradition. The blood brotherhood rites strengthen egalitarianism even among unrelated neighbors. Evans-Pritchard described the rites among the Azande in Central Africa where the ceremony strengthens existing bonds, gives them more concrete form, and provides heavy negative sanctions for failure to act according to one's oath. Blood brotherhood gives to the more tenuous sentiment of friendship a status comparable to that of close kin relationship. It enlarges the kin relationship because it spreads the kinship obligations to non-kin.[18]

The blood brother demands assistance when the brother is in need. Failure to act in accordance with your blood oath brings the curse of the blood on you. Blood brothers are exhorted to protect each other, each other's children, wives, and possessions, and to share worldly goods and food with the brother in need. Blood brotherhood introduces more rather than less equality, not as in clan relationships where hierarchical relationships still exist (i.e., an elder brother, younger brother, etc).[19]

And it is an equality within poverty. Sara Berry wrote in 1993 that low-income farmers have more trouble coping with risk, not because they are innately conservative, but because they are poor. Because they have few assets and little or no credit to tide them over periods of poor harvest or shortfalls in income, they often choose crops, methods of production or off-farm activities likely to yield income at regular, short intervals, rather than those which might yield higher returns, but only at longer or less regular intervals. In this respect, African farmers are like poor farmers in other parts of the world.[20]   Indeed, a decade ago the vast majority of Africa's population remained in low-productivity agriculture so that there was essentially no chance of economic development.   The UN Food and Agriculture Organization estimated that 68.2 percent of Africa's total population was in agriculture compared to 56.5 percent for all developing countries, and that by the year 2000 this percentage would only have dropped to 62.6 percent (compared to 50.6 percent for all developing countries).[21]

So, as a general rule, we have poor, subsistence, parochial farmers infected with misplaced altruism in the form of kinship obligations sometimes called the extended family that equalize rather than permit the social divisions that prefigure modernization. A modern example from the Ivory Coast focused on two business partners in a tailor shop who lamented their kinship obligations, which they described as the steady importunings of unemployed relatives who prevented them from accumulating any savings. They bought schoolbooks and uniforms for nieces and nephews, paid medical fees for sick relatives, and opened their wallets for everything from burials, to ceaseless requests for "dépannage," or simply a bit of financial help. Refusal, they argued, reminding one of the penalties for not helping a blood brother or his family, carried with it the risk of being cursed.

If you earn five francs, they said, ten people, both relatives and friends, will ask you to share it with them. The two tailors felt that they were suffering death by one-thousand nicks, and they were tempted to ask: Why bother to work?[22]

Despite the evidence of this misplaced altruism (kinship obligations), which prevents development in the western sense, it is ignored. Black Africa is described as developing, backward, and needing an economic assistance that does more than create an indigenous elite in tune with the White man's world, while the majority of the population is untouched. The observer's improper reading of the action of modernization in the first place seems to prevent an acknowledgement that misplaced altruism, the extension of rural equality beyond its historical utility, can fundamentally hamstring agriculture and with it the sort of class separation on which modernization depends. So the actual modernization that does develop in such societies is stunted, malnourished, and resistant to the notion of a centralized state, while at the same time preventing intervening layers of society between the rich and the poor, creating the prerequisites for tyranny.

This hypothesis can also be tested in a situation very different from the kinship system of Black Africa. The second example is Russia in the last few centuries, with particular reference to the serf population in the nineteenth century and to the collective farm population in the twentieth century. Misplaced altruism was present in the serf egalitarianism that was enforced in both the nineteenth and twentieth centuries.

Alexander Yanov suggested in 1987 that this egalitarianism was a deliberate effort made by counter-reformers who sought to maintain Russia's medieval political system. These enemies of progress knew, he argued, that in Europe the main means of dismantling such a political system was through the creation of a strong middle class. They favored, therefore, whatever stood in the way of or prevented its development.

> As European history shows, the creation of a strong middle class depends, in the first instance, on the differentiation of the peasantry, and it is this that had to be forcibly stopped. Serfdom, the peasant commune, and the collectivization of agriculture were all different means of artificially keeping the peasantry in its medieval state.[23]

Peasant enserfment was a process that occurred between the thirteenth and fifteenth centuries, from the 1200s to the 1400s, when the peasants were gradually enslaved. Peasants or rural workers were first turned into tenants on very large estates. Contributing factors were the growth of landholding by princes, church, and boyars, which reduced the number of small farmers, all of whom were peasant; taxation privileges given to large estate owners acted as a magnet drawing peasants from local areas to the estate that had the tax privileges; restrictions that limited the tenant's right to give up his tenancy kept the peasant in a status where taxes had to be paid and where part of the produce had to be given to the lord; and, finally, increasing peasant indebtedness tied them to one place. The peasant paid taxes, paid rent for the land and use of farm buildings and obtained subsidies from the lord at high interest rates. As a free peasant, he could leave the tenancy, but not until his debt was paid.[24]

Over the years, even this freedom was taken away. Moving away was discouraged and then prohibited by law. Enserfment was complete by 1649, and the class so enslaved was over 70 percent of the Russian population.

In 1678, the male population of Russia, excluding the newly acquired left—bank Ukraine and the Baltic areas, was about 5 million. A total of 90 percent or about 4.36 million of these males were peasants, of which 53.5

percent or 2.3 million were privately held, 16.3 percent or .7 million worked land owned by the Russian Orthodox Church, 9.3 percent or .4 million were classed as court peasants, and 20.9 percent or .9 million were called state peasants. If one restricts the word "serf" to the first two classes, the serfs made up seven-tenths of the peasant population. Over the years the .9 million state peasants became "almost serfs," particularly after they were channelled into communes in 1838.[25] This process, which resulted in the consolidation of the Russian population into two dominant classes, was a gradual process probably only dimly recognized by the participants.[26] In 1782, the percentage of the Russian male population called noble was less than 1 percent (.79 percent). This changed slightly when Poland was acquired and provided more land to create more nobles, but basically it did not move too far from 1 percent.[27]

Although the earlier decrees had created serfdom by restricting movement, the noble landlords wasted no time in acting as if they actually owned the peasants who lived on their lands, and a series of acts pushed by the Tsars and Tsarinas made it clear that they did. The condition of the Russian serfs thus deteriorated sharply, and by the middle of the 1700s the formal power of the landlord over his serfs was akin to the power of the American plantation owner over his slaves.[28]

Ever more tied to the land the Russian serf became quite different from peasants in Europe that were increasingly released from the ties that held them to specific land.

> As serfdom spread and became recognized as the fate of most peasants, the multiplicity of divisions that differentiated the laboring population became meaningless and gradually evaporated.[29]

Communal egalitarianism for the serfs reinforced the interests of the state, and, therefore, the state conspired to resist rural stratification, the enemy of the communal way of life.[30] Rural stratification in Russia was thus very slow to develop up to 1850, and after that stratification was minimal, as in the difference between a family with one horse and a family with two.[31] Confirmation that this existing, limited stratification did not alter the serfs' basic communal outlook, sense of shared values, or common interests was best seen in their collective behavior during risings in the late nineteenth century.[32]

Emancipation finally came in 1861. If the goal of the Emancipation Statute was to end the personal bondage of serf to master, it was in large part successful. If the goal were to create capitalized agriculture, it never left the starting blocks. Large amounts of the landlord's land may have been given to the peasants to work as their own, but they had to pay for that land. The charge was distributed over a forty-nine year period at 6 percent interest. Village communes were charged with the responsibility of distributing this land to local peasants as well as collecting their payments for it. This new role for the communes reduced their significance as a force for democracy and made them little more than efficient collection agencies for the state.

What does all this have to do with harmful altruism? Just this. Progressive enserfment reinforced an egalitarianism in Russian village life and preserved it well beyond its historical utility. This was accomplished by the following methods:[33]

1. The manner of allocating land to work teams from the village economically pressured people to stay together in three generation households ruled by the patriarch. The less successful would be aided by the more successful in the extended family structure. Striking out on one's own did not make economic sense for the landlord or the peasant because of the high risk of failure. This high sense of risk when going out on one's own needs to be remembered when describing Russian farmers in the 1990s as also rather unwilling to move in the directions of really private farming. Their history has been to reduce alleged risks by collective labor, whether that be by extended family or the organization of the collective farm, however inefficient these may have been.

2. Land to farm and rights to pasture as well as to corvée assignments (unpaid labor for the landlord or the state if one was a state peasant) were handled by the village commune elders in such a way as to maximize equality rather than to further the careers of the successful farmers. Because the land was owned by the frequently absentee lord, one could not "get ahead" by gaining more land than someone else. A little cheating was possible but not the acquisition of land.

3. Troublemakers were put on the recruitment list or exiled to Siberia. Frequently, maybe once a year, the military recruiter came through the area and stopped off at the village to see whether the village elders had put anyone on the list. If so, the individual was taken for service in the military for the normal period of twenty-five years. This kept people in line.

4. In times of crisis when a crop might be bad and hunger would thin out the ranks of the unsuccessful, estate grain reserves were used while they were available to supplement the peasant's diet, and after the crisis loans would be made to those who had lost their horses, so even natural disasters were not allowed to create a differentiation.

The former legal bondage, in other words, became economic bondage after 1861. The former serfs were still tied to narrow strips of land, but now they could not hope to get better strips next year, and, with no education, and even less agricultural technology, the Emancipation Edict foreclosed any real growth in agricultural technology. When this was coupled with population growth in the rural areas that resulted in even less land per person, both of the main economic purposes behind the Emancipation were frustrated; the possibilities of surplus crops for the growing cities and surplus labor for the growing industrialization.

Remedies were slow in coming. The poll tax, levied on every male peasant and representing about 45 percent of the collected tax in the 1880s, was repealed in 1887. To compensate the state for this loss, however, the excise on spirits was increased and redemption payments extended to the category of former state peasants. So one hand stopped taking while the other hand took in different ways. A real remedy, nonetheless, was enacted on November 3, 1905 when all redemption payments were canceled. From 1905, twelve years of relative freedom and growth were seriously set back by three years of civil war during which grain was forcibly extracted by the Bolsheviks, and then in 1921 agriculture was free again for about seven years until 1928 when it was smashed by collectivization. Sixty-seven years after emancipation the peasants were once again serfs tied this time to the collective farm. The intervening time period was far too short to unravel centuries of structure and tradition. The starting point was too low and incentives were most unclear. Nonetheless progress was made and the beginnings of rural stratification did become visible, only to be smashed again by collectivization. Even though rich peasants (*kulaki*) were mainly an imaginary class created by Stalin to provide a class enemy, there were some rich peasants in 1927 and another fifty years could have seen dramatic rural change.

Stalin began the collectivization of agriculture with great suddenness in 1928. The reason was not ideological, that is, he did not push the Soviet Union in this direction because he wanted the countryside to be more communistic. The reasons had more to do with control of the countryside and the need to extract agricultural surpluses from the rural areas without rural opposition.

The countryside had undergone tremendous changes since the Bolsheviks took over in 1917. The large estates, from which surpluses could be regularly expected, had been eliminated by peasant unrest. The result was a strong movement away from large estates to approximately 25.5 million individual peasant farms. Most of these were small farms of less than thirty acres and they tended to be underequipped and inefficiently run.[34] Surpluses of grain were less evident, and with so many peasant farmers involved it proved difficult to keep them in line. During the mid 1920s, therefore, farmers began to learn the old lessons of withholding grain from the market so as to force up the price. The cities needed to be fed, but Stalin also needed agricultural surpluses to export in order to pay for industrial imports.

In December 1927, Stalin ordered that force be used to extract grain from peasant hoarders, and early the next year he ordered the forced collectivization of the rural areas of the Soviet Union. Of the approximately 25 million peasant farms, about 24 percent were run by poor peasants who in general possessed neither livestock or tools. The largest group, about 72 percent, was made up of middle peasants who had comfortable livings and wanted no radical changes. Only about 4 percent were the rich peasants or *kulaki*; industrious and prosperous farmers who wanted no part of collectivization.[35]

The only peasants who welcomed the collectivization were those who had something to gain from the move to collective farms. All those, whether middle or rich peasants, who had livestock and tools of their own, saw collectivization as a loss of individual property to the collective. These latter folk tended to resist collectivization, and all resisters were labeled *kulaki*.

The collectivization of agriculture in the Soviet Union, therefore, quickly became a class war against the successful: the middle and rich peasants who resisted. The ideology was used not only to mask the systematic murder of millions of people in the name of the dream of a better future, but was also used to mask the greed of the poor peasants who were promised the cattle and equipment of the middle and rich peasants who were killed or moved away in boxcars, like unvalued cattle, with a one-way ticket to a gulag in Siberia.

The chaotic result of these policies was the systematic uprooting of the most productive and efficient farmers and preventing their return; coupled with a forcible extraction of grain by the state that often left none to be sown as seed in the following year. Famine, caused by Stalin's short-sighted stubbornness, cost millions of lives particularly in Ukraine. Cannibalism ironically returned to the black earth area that was so rich in agricultural potential. The drive to collectivize slowed a bit in 1930 but never really stopped, and by 1938 some 93.5 percent of all farms were collectivized.[36]

The brutal collectivization campaign benefitted no one: not the state, nor the farms, nor the peasants. Because they did not want to lose their animals or machinery to the collective, peasants frequently slaughtered and ate their animals and destroyed their tools before coming to the collective. Ironically, some died from overeating, while millions died from famine. But the net result was that the collective did not receive the livestock or the machinery. What was shared was poverty. Although the government introduced the death penalty for destroying livestock or machinery, the collectives started from very poor levels and were, for several decades, systematically underfinanced by a state eager to purchase industrialization with agricultural produce no matter what the cost to agriculture or to people who needed food to survive. As a result the collective agriculture in the Soviet Union remained a poor relation and stratification never resulted.

This enforced egalitarianism endured until 1991. After removing the collective structure from agriculture, there was some comment that there were very few risk takers willing to lead Russian agriculture into a capitalized future. That should have been no surprise. The class on the ground was not in the time frame of the expectation.

This has happened elsewhere, as Johan Huizinga demonstrated. This also highlights the question raised by de Tocqueville: whether or not liberal democracy can develop when one of its significant precursors is left out of the equation. The answer appears to be no. Harmful altruism causes fairly permanent damage.

NOTES

1. See the discussion in John Dunn, *Western Political Theory in the Face of the Future* (Cambridge: Cambridge University Press, 1993), pp. 6–9. The de Tocqueville reference, p. 9.

2. Johan Huizinga, The Autumn of the Middle Ages, p. 61.

3. Ibid., pp. 63, 64.

4. David McLellan, *Karl Marx, His Life and Thought* (New York: Harper and Row, 1973, p. 212.

5. David Hume, *Treatise of Human Nature*, Book II, Part II, Sec. 6 (London: Everyman's Library, 1737).

6. Frederick Watkins, *Hume: Theory of Politics* (Austin, TX: University of Texas Press, 1953), p. xxv.

7. Details from Lady Musgrove Island are drawn from personal experience on that coral island in February 1998.

8. Lucy Mair, *African Societies* (London: Cambridge University Press, 1974), p. 1.

9. Ibid., p. 2.

10. E. Wayne Nafziger, "Japan's Industrial Development, 1868–1939: Lessons for Sub-Saharan Africa," in Howard Stein, ed., *Asian Industrialization and Africa: Studies in Policy Alternatives to Structural Adjustment* (New York: St. Martin's Press, 1995), p. 53.

11. Raymond Firth, *Economics of the New Zealand Maori* (Wellington: R. E. Owen, Government Printer, 1959), p. 492. Obviously Firth's work predates considerably the process of returning the land to the Maori that began in 1995.

12. Ibid., p. 493.

13. Ibid.

14. Ibid., p. 3.

15. Ibid., p. 6.

16. Evan E. Evans-Pritchard, Raymond Firth, et al., *The Institutions of Primitive Society* (Glencoe, IL: The Free Press, 1959), pp. 63–64.

17. P. Robson and D.A. Lury, eds., *The Economies of Africa* (Evanston, IL: Northwestern University Press, 1969), p. 39.

18. Evan E. Evans-Pritchard, *Essays in Social Anthropology* (New York: The Free Press of Glencoe, 1963), pp. 131ff.

19. Ibid., p. 159.

20.   Sara Berry, "Coping with Confusion: African Farmers' Responses to Economic Instability in the 1970s and 1980s," in Thomas M. Callaghy and John Ravenhill, eds., *Hemmed-In: Responses to Africa's Economic Decline* (New York: Columbia University Press, 1993), p. 249.

21. Jeffrey Herbst, in ibid., p. 336. The author is quoting from the *FAO Quarterly Bulletin of Statistics*, 2, 3 [1989]: pp. 21-25.

22.   Howard W. French, "Does Sharing Wealth Only Promote Poverty?" *The New York Times*, January 14, 1995, p. 4.

23.   Alexander Yanov, *The Russian Challenge and the Year 2000*, Iden J. Rosenthal, trans. (New York: Basil Blackwell, 1987), p. 216.

24. Ibid., p. 415.

25. Ibid., pp. 27–39. The edict that created the communes for state peasants was "The Regulation for the Administration of the State Domains in the Provinces."   See Basil Dmytryshyn, *A History of Russia* (Engelwood Cliffs, NJ: Prentice-Hall, 1977), pp. 347–348. After emancipation in 1861 state peasants were given twice the land normal serfs were granted and required to pay about one-half of the serf's redemption payment. Hence the "almost serf." Ibid., p. 336.

26. Ibid., p. 36.

27. Kolchin, p. 40.

28. Ibid., p. 50.

29. Ibid., p. 37.

30. Ibid., p. 339.

31. Ibid., pp. 340–341.

32. Ibid., p. 34.

33.   See Steven L. Hoch, *Serfdom and Social Control in Russia: Petrovskoe, a Village in Tambov* (Chicago: University of Chicago Press, 1986), Chapters 3 and 4, or pp. 117ff, 136ff.

34. Basil Dmytryshyn, *A History of Russia*, p. 534.

35. Ibid.

36. Ibid., p. 535.

Chapter 9

Altruism and the Environment

The unfamiliar word *eco-altruism* is simply a rather pompous way of saying that any decent discussion of altruism should also include references to the connections between that human–animal virtue and the world that surrounds them, going well beyond and expanding the word *social* so that eco-altruism comes to mean doing something for the environment at some cost to oneself. Environmental selfishness, contrarily, is just as simple a topic: doing something for oneself at the expense of the environment.

In order for these apparently simple ideas to make sense to anyone, it should be demonstrated that humans and the environment are just as irrevocably connected as humans and other humans. We cannot get away from the environment any more than can the fish or the lion or the cow. And yet, people have no trouble ignoring it. But it cannot be ignored for much longer. Our ignorance of how it all fits together will kill us. It is rather like being up in space and discovering that one's space suit has a leak. The space suit is the only friendly environment, standing between the person and the unfriendly environment outside—and if it is steadily eroding the astronaut is in real difficulty. Our lack of awareness of the interconnectedness similarly erodes our support systems as we pollute the water we drink, the food we eat, the soil we plant, and the air we breathe.

Not enough people seem to be cognizant of these connections. So when one stumbles on someone else speaking the same language it is a very pleasant surprise. A person who writes a gardening column for the local newspaper is not a likely source to exhibit these interconnections, and yet that is precisely where it could be found on a foggy Saturday morning in late January. Janet Macunovich, an advanced master gardener, raised an ethical question regarding a matter introduced by a reader: Should you raise areas that are wet in spring because you don't like to see all the water on the ground? Her answer described the local interconnections to the bothered letter writer (i.e., low spots being natural sinks that hold water and silt in the area and the other things that need that temporary additional water). Macunovich then wrote that if

> altruism doesn't prompt you to let seeping land
> lie, consider the trees and other plants that you
> value in that natural area. They are probably
> species that evolved in seasonally wet conditions
> and may rely on that extra moisture for their
> continued good health.[1]

Nature, she wrote, may not always be pretty but it works without maintenance. The problem could be solved in ensuing springs simply by turning one's head for a few days while the water soaked in.[2]

Eco-altruism, in this instance, simply involved turning one's head for a few days and allowing nature to handle the water that briefly lay atop the soil. The trigger for the altruism in this instance, as in most others dealing with the environment, is the awareness of interconnectedness, an intermeshing that includes the observer. Everything is a part of everything else. This is so obvious a fact that it seems incredible that people do not understand it from the cradle. Why is interconnectedness so hidden? Why does one feel like a practitioner of an Eastern religion when talking about so obvious a fact?

Because in the Western world science could only develop when scholastic and rigid religious beliefs about the reality of universals were discredited. The view that abstractions were objectively real, that universals were more than names, had to be countered by the denial of empiricalness to the non-empirical, and thus science developed in an ambience of separation and distinctness. Discreet phenomena were the only ones admitted. Early scientists had to pull so hard to distinguish the phenomenon from the noumenon (the empirical appearance from the thing in itself) in order to ascribe reality to appearance in what was called "nominalism," but they threw the interconnectedness "baby" out with the "universals are real" bath water. They ignored the noumena lying behind the phenomena. This deepened an existing alienation from God, nature, other humans, and oneself.

It was already deep. We were so alienated from God that, in Christianity at least, a part of God was said to die to make us whole. Yet whole we did not become. Alienation persisted and so a church organization arose ostensibly to solve the problem by bridging the gap between God and human, but in reality the church formed to join together the alienated. It seemed to make sense but did not. Religion's goal was to reconnect us but it failed for the most part because the church maintained the separation. We worshipped a far off deity through rituals that came to have lives of their own. We were taught that God loved us, but we were not taught to love, and people didn't change. The separation sin, selfishness, was forgiven but the healing power of loving connectedness remained unknown. Church leaders, people in general, just did not know that receiving the love of God is not nearly as important as giving one's own love to God (however described) and to all of God's creatures. That would have brought the connectedness. The Gospel writer Mark wrote that a scribe asked Jesus which was the most important commandment, and it seemed that there were two, and not just one. The first was to love God wholly, and a second, like it, was to love one's neighbor as oneself. The person asking the question now said that keeping these two commandments was more important than all the rituals in use and Jesus agreed (Mk 12:30-34).

Philosophies, as we have seen, also tried to overcome alienation, but they missed the point as well. Hegelianism spent volumes of words trying to convince people that they were part of the Absolute and of every other thing in the world as well. The sin here was to see things as Other, as distinct from oneself. The base or cause of the sin of separation, selfishness, was not comprehended. Karl Marx materialized this Hegelian idealism by describing Hegel's historical progress a la Ludwig Feuerbach,[3] as a history of human production that would eventually overcome alienation by the proletarian revolution and by socializing the means of production. This great push toward equality not only ignored the human craving for liberty but also failed to address the real problem: relying on the magic of the socialization of the means of production was not going to change the inner human condition. In the twinkling of an eye, people were expected to turn from grasping and taking to giving and sharing.

Altruism is a major step toward furthering that togetherness between human and deity, human and human, and human and the rest of the world. It is about the only step that makes sense when one thinks of environmental needs because it is the only "ism" that will reach out and pull together the strands of connectedness that bind us.

Communism, commune-ism or social-ism, incredibly failed to create an awareness of interconnectedness. The loving and the caring of real people for their sisters and brothers, their environments, and their deities were lost from sight as communism became the pursuit of productive wealth instead of the sharing society.[4] The basic reason for this was that communism very quickly came to be simply another form of capitalism, and because they were communist capitalists they felt they had to "catch up"; they polluted the earth, sky, and water even more than regular capitalists did. Travel through eastern Europe and Russia if you like, but in many areas wear a mask.

Christianity's and communism's main goal should have been overcoming the alienation between humans and all other things both high and low, but they have not understood their mission very well. Failing to move against selfishness by living, not preaching, altruism, both the church and

communist parties allowed self-interest to reign, and alienation went untreated
while preaching worsened the situation by talking about the problem rather
than the solution.

The result, of course, is that alienation was never properly addressed,
and one very strong side of it is the way in which the world of nature does not
appear to us as a part of our very existence, but as an Other, as an Object that
can be treated in isolation from ourselves so that it fits our perception of short-
term gratification. So when we drive a tanker truck full of toxic chemicals
into the middle of a field late at night and open all the valves to discharge the
poisons, we are not hurting anything, we say. We are only short-circuiting
those stupid state laws that interfere with the way real men make their money.
Dumping sewage into the river? Pouring sulfur oxides into the air to make
acid rain? Raping the land to seize coal near the surface? Building housing
developments on prime agricultural land? The list could go on for a long time
because our sense of connection with nature is not there. We just do not see
the connections that are right before our eyes.

For example, take a very visible, nonphilosophical look at rainfall, the
kind that might interfere with a simple picnic. Some 80 percent of the solar
energy that reaches the earth is used to evaporate water from the oceans, lakes,
and streams of the planet. Water ascends as vapor, forms lovely looking
clouds, reaches the coolness of the upper air and falls back to earth as rain.
This is nature's way (God's way if you like) of irrigating the land, but about
75 percent of this rain falls back into the ocean. Because only about 16
percent of the evaporated water comes from the land, there is a beneficial
water transfer from the oceans to the land. More water evaporates from the
oceans than returns to them as rain and the difference falls on the land. It has
been estimated that the positive difference for the land areas is about 40,000
cubic kilometers, a very critical difference because nature is transferring water
from a non-useful (in this narrow context), saline condition to the fresh water
category and allowing the land to receive more water than it itself gives in
evaporation. Total annual evaporation from the oceans was estimated at
430,000 cubic kilometers while precipitation over oceans was 390,000.[5]

The connections do not end there. Only about 25 percent of this
ocean augmented rainfall falls on land, and it does not always come when it
is needed. If the prevailing winds change direction because there is too much
dust or smoke in the air the local climate can change permanently. If the rain
being diverted is one of many throughout the year the damage may be slight,
but if the rain is the annual monsoon that is diverted by the changed winds,
then economic ruin can come to an entire nation.

Monsoons are created by winds formed by the heated air near the
equator that flow north and south from the intertropical discontinuity, which
is created by the shifting position of the earth in relation to the sun. If the
shifted winds cross oceans they bring water. If they only cross land they

remain dry. Sometimes the shift in monsoon winds is caused by the presence or absence of the "westerlies" or prevailing out-of-the-west winds formed by the Coriolis Force. If the westerlies are too far to the south (wintertime) or too far to the north (summertime) they may block the monsoon winds.[6] And so forth and so on; the interconnections are global.

An example of the global connections is summed up by the word *teleconnection*, which describes poorly understood relations between "events" very distant from each other. For example, a higher than normal atmospheric pressure over Darwin, Australia, correlates with above normal temperatures in Duluth, Minnesota, and below normal temperatures in the southern United States. The teleconnection signal is passed by warm ocean water. This is an example of balance in a functioning system, but to describe what the relating is does not imply an ability to explain the why of it. Intense, invisible connection, but very, very real.[7]

But there are other connections that complicate the issue even further, other environments as well in which earthly life finds itself enmeshed. For example, one can speak of *ecospirituality*, where the word draws attention to the need to walk in the ambience of some spirit, say the spirit of God, and implies a strong spiritual element tying together the human and the environment with a divine power. Ecospirituality, as in the works of Thomas Berry, seeks to make visible the ties between earth, humans, and the deity. A different dimension of this ecospirituality is the barely acknowledged space occupied when a person is in touch with the deity and apparently out of the existential world at least mentally. This is a space having a different "form of reality," perhaps simply the area of silence noted by Wittgenstein.[8] Other dimensions of the concept are, for example, *ecofeminism*, a word coined in 1974 by the French feminist author, Francoise d'Eaubonne, which draws attention to the connections between life-giving, endangered, and exploited nature and life-giving, endangered, and exploited women; *ecobiology*, or a new biology that stresses the relations between living organisms and their living and nonliving environment; and *ecosociology*, which describes the relation between the distribution of human groups with reference to material resources and consequent social and cultural patterns. Putting all these together may be unwise. The most recent all-embracing philosophies like Hegelianism and Marxism and possibly feminism have not succeeded in accomplishing this goal. Alienation in the three theoretical systems was easily discovered to be the cause of the problem, but it was removable only in theory. So long as Hegel, Marx, and feminists looked backward, values remained invariant because nothing that was not accounted for in the theory got in the way; but projecting forward, where theory faced implementation in the empirical world, the fine lines of theory began to blur. The theoretical map was not the territory, and because it was not, the territory surprised the mapmakers. Hegelianism and Marxism and possibly feminism depended on an uncritical acceptance of rationalizations that did not describe the interconnectedness that they should have matched. The hill on the map was a dale in the territory. A theory of interconnectedness can similarly be an out of touch map. One needs to examine the fit between theory and what it purports to describe.

This interconnectedness provides the basis for altruism in the sense that if the major altruistic motivator is need in another, one has to be at least dimly aware of the interconnection to feel the need. But this relating is not easily discussed. The interrelationship one seeks to investigate is almost deliberately hidden at times. Invariant separateness, such as the caricature of individualism popularized by Ayn Rand, became the rule long ago as humans learned to objectify nature and to treat the world as their playground. Science and the scientific approach, which van Nieuwenhuijze called a subtle lie,[9] led us to value only that which could be measured and continued the medieval dualism that unnecessarily separated spirit and matter, mind and body, soul and body, light and dark, good and evil, and heaven and earth.

In addition, interconnectedness is difficult to discuss because it is so very complicated. Charles Darwin told the story about the relation between the number of cats in a district and the yield of red clover in the fields. Red clover is pollinated only by bumblebees, because no other insect can reach the nectar; so if the bees became extinct so would the red clover. This is a straightforward relationship easy to understand. But it can get more complicated, quite easily. Bumblebees are the desired prey of field mice who eat their larvae and destroy their nests. So if field mice are on the increase in a district, both the bumblebees and red clover will diminish. But the number of field mice is related to the number of cats, and so the number of cats in a district should be an indicator of how much red clover could be seen in the fields.[10] Going beyond this story, Reid suggested that because single females were more likely to own cats, the number of single females in a district should correlate tightly with the amount of red clover. If the marriage rates rose, presumably the red clover rates would decrease.

The complications in this story are fun, but Reid suggested that it was superficial because there were still so many other factors involved in the particulars of the red clover story. The interconnectedness, for example, is not only horizontal, but vertical as well. Reid argued that to have a grasp of the total environment, one needed to understand the five levels of ecological organizational linkage: organisms whether plant or animal, population groups of individuals or one species, community containing all population groups in an area ecosystem (the sum of all communities plus non-living environs), and biosphere (the sum total of all life on earth).[11]

Augustine, relying on the ancient Stoics, saw a similar layering of interconnecting levels: households, city-states or political systems, earth, and universe. The inclusion of the dear departed and angels who may be future souls gave Augustine both a time-backward and a time-forward connectedness as well: a form of transcendent connection. The ability to complicate interconnectedness, thus, has a long history.

For example, do the interconnections between people and their environment arise because of some internal purpose? Some internal or external force acting on the connecting parts? A mechanistic or deterministic understanding of the universe, such as in Jean Calvin's predestination, suggests that people do not interact out of conscious purpose or choice so much as they are driven to action by internal and external forces. So the interconnection would not be consciously sought under these conditions. Even sociobiology fell into this pit. In his book *The Selfish Gene*, Richard Dawkins had people driven by their genes, and not for their own purposes so much as that of their genes. People became bodies for genes to operate in this analysis, robots like Calvin's "determined" saints. Springing out of or escaping the determinism is as difficult as springing free from religion or absolute goals. It can, however, be done. The categorical imperative may demand, but the human response can be chosen rather than be automatically one or the other. Freedom is a defining characteristic of the human.

And, as if this were not enough complexity, we also have a long history in not knowing what is being interconnected when we interact. We have been assuming the reality of endpoints in our interconnectedness theories that are either reifications or badly understood reality. For example, the old biology of Darwin, Wallace, Huxley, and Tennyson, which saw a competitive nature, red in tooth and claw, does not square with biologists' observations of nature.[12] It is rare, for instance, for two animals to struggle over the same piece of meat. Competition in nature is normally avoided by walking away, by the division of the habitat into niches, by different species eating different foods, eating at different times of the day, or eating at different heights on the tree as in Robert MacArthur's study of five species of warblers living in the same coniferous Maine forest.[13]

Nature cooperates more than it competes, whereas humans compete more than cooperate. But even this statement is misleading. On average, women may compete less than men, and some parts of the world seem less inclined to compete compared to other parts where there seems to be a competitive eagerness. To the extent that red in tooth and claw describes anything it seems to suggest the behavior of some animals some of the time and possibly some humans, located mainly in societies where violence is encouraged either by a high degree of poverty or high levels of hatred.

Part of the problem in comprehending the "what" that connects is that we deal with an imaginary nature. Carl von Weizacker wrote that the physical worldview of the nineteenth century took the forms of our perception in so far as they corresponded to classical physics, as absolute, and therefore thought that a process that was not perceptible to the senses had been understood only when it had been reduced to a model after the pattern of the perceptible. We recognized how this conception, too, derives from the thought of a unified picture of the world. We see what we think we should see.[14]

The same is hopefully not true in what is called new biology. Augros and Stanciu wrote that the new biology began with what is known and now observable. It did not require us to impose anything artificial onto nature. Too much of the present regime, they said, began with an imaginary nature. It searched nature for things it expected to see but which were not there, such as ill-adapted organisms, competition, and rational thought and language in animals.[15]

The continual expectation of what is not there brings about a blindness to what is found in nature: cooperation among organisms, purposefulness, efficiency, and harmony with the environment. These are either ignored or resolved to their opposites by having recourse to an unobservable hypothetical past like a state of nature. We are unable, therefore, to see what nature is, and we imagine her to be many things she is not. This is the opposite of good science. "But the nature we have discovered is a model for both engineer and artist. Her attributes of simplicity, economy, beauty, purpose, and harmony make her a model for ethics and politics."[16]

It is difficult to communicate this because our language is not equipped to do so. Maurice Ash argued that we have lost the language, the language of myth, in which our forebears made sense of what we call environment. Myths with all their teeming deities, peopled the regions we now characterize as environment.

Among the ancient Maya, for example, there were specific deities; male and female, animal and human, associated with corn, death, decay, the moon, Venus, mountains, divine lineage, and many other themes. In addition, the Maya believed in companion spirits or co-essences, an animal form that accompanied each person through life like a guardian angel.[17] We do not need a new series of myths in order to describe an ecology of interconnectedness; that would probably be counterproductive. Berry wrote that what we need to do is recreate the language of relationships so as to express our connections. Although Berry's idea may result in a romanticizing of connections, relation words are available. My mother the sun, and so forth. He thought that we have forgotten relationship language and that we can no longer hear the voices nor speak in response.[18] What we need, he argued, is a re-enchantment with the earth. To carry this out effectively, we must now, in a sense, reinvent the human as a species within the community of life species. Our sense of reality and of value must consciously shift from an anthropocentric to an ecocentric norm of reference.[19]

A more compelling reason for language difficulty than a loss of the language of myth (Ash) or a language of relationship (Berry) is that the language we use is a language of existence, pivoting on the atom, depending on the substances to which we have reduced the world. The language of substance or existence is inadequate for interdependence because it is the language of causation and reflects the atomized discreetness that pulls against connectiveness.[20] The language in use is one of existence only, not of essence. To say the same thing in Kantian words, we have a language of phenomena but not of noumena, nor of the different form of reality in Wittgenstein's silence. The attracting value of interconnectedness thus runs into the mine field of a language unable to handle the value, and the attraction that could pull us away from alienation disappears.

Even though limited, our language of existence seeks universal applicability. It forces a reification of the noumenal world, and primitively insists on overdefining the interconnected parts, creating a false sense of subject-object relations. This happened centuries ago with theology. As a result the vital, spiritual interconnectedness in the transcendent area was squeezed by perverted religions into a dichotomous, subject–object relation with a reified deity. Both subject and objects were skewed because our essential self, the subject, was not a substance either, but a metaphysical olio of processes. If we do not pay attention, this is what the language of existence does very easily: thingify what is not a thing. Instead of understanding that and dealing with it we create a theory of interconnectedness from a skewed vision of reality in which both subject and object are misunderstood.

We are as careless when we speak of the environment. We objectify it, treating as thing what is a different form of reality in the world of essence, a form in which we move and that gives us life and meaning and possibility. To argue that there are different forms of reality is to argue (as do Ash and Wittgenstein) that words do not define objects; that their meanings lie in their use, in all its kaleidoscopic variety. We, as users of words, are not solitary intelligences, with no other function than to think; we are constituted of our every day interactions with one another, and it is as much our feelings as our intellects that compose us.[21]

This confusion means that we need to leave childish thinking with its need for objects and definitions so as to feel the excitement of dealing with what is really there, or not there because we are a part of what we observe. We are a part of a totality called environment, essentially indivisible. If we

> separate out one part of our environment, we
> must in so doing engage with it instrumentally,
> and to us it will then cease to be the environ-
> ment of our actions and become a component of
> them. Environment is that which our intentional
> actions themselves are not.[22]

Yet, Ash continued, there is neither calculus nor rule to guide these instincts. The scientific method does not apply. Indeed, its forced application makes us ill. Like a sick animal that cures itself by seeking a different herbage, we turn away from it. But because all we understand is the possession of things, we make ourselves worse. An environment cannot be possessed.[23]

Part of our problem is that the environment is not measurable, it is not discrete nor a material substance. It is not definable because it has no finite boundaries with the world. But it certainly is real in some fashion. What the West takes for objects is what the East takes for conveniences of speech. We in the West are too object oriented. Perhaps the world is better understood in terms of relationships rather than of separate substances. Perhaps environmental relations are better understood as the balancing, regenerative actions implicit in yinning and yanging.[24]

In other words, instead of continuing to refine the map we might try dealing with the territory itself. This may help us appreciate the mystery of the environment, lying as it does beyond the mechanistic explanations on the boundaries of speech. Ash reminded us that Wittgenstein, however much he sounded like a positivist at first, passionately believed that all that really mattered in life was precisely what, in his view, we must be silent about.[25] Palmer wrote that positivists reacted to Wittgenstein's statement by muttering "He's a mystic."[26]

David Hume showed long ago that we impose an order on the world through our language, an order that is not there without the language. Kant demonstrated a short time later in his *Critique of Pure Reason* that the language of existence cannot describe the essential or noumenal world. Instead of cherishing human inarticulateness in the face of the transcendent, in our arrogance we pretend that noumena are "real" so as to bring them into the phenomenological world. But to imagine success in this endeavor is to have nothing about which to be silent; it is to use language to justify domination, to sanction hierarchies of power and to assume, arrogantly, that we are God.

Because we have only the language of existence, we cannot easily speak of whatever is in the world of essence. What we are silent about has no reference. It is neither a nothing nor a something. This understanding of the limits of speech, the limits of reason, and the difference between cause and regularity (Hume) may be the hinge on which the doors of our civilization could turn.

The environment is not synonymous with nature because it includes social worlds as well as physical worlds. With this understanding, to say that the environment is out of balance means much more than the words ecological crisis appear to mean. Sensing this larger environmental context allows one to appreciate how interwoven ecological crises are with gender and social domination. Rosemary Radford Ruether said these ecological crises had their beginnings in the structures of power and ownership. The exploitation of natural resources occurs through the domination of labor, which necessitates the domination of the bodies of some people by other people.

> The abuse of the resources of the earth becomes acute when a small ruling class, who establish ownership and control of land, people and techniques, can use the labour of the vast majority of people to extract these resources, but without having to take into consideration their rights and needs as human persons.[27]

The operating assumption, she argued, of such a pattern of industrialization through gender and social domination is that profits must be maximized for the owners. And that means minimized for the nonowners. And, of course, the owners, the affluent in the society, seek to solve ecological problems without in any way changing or challenging the system of gender and social domination that is its underlying presupposition. This is what Rosalind Miles meant when she wrote that

> the arrogant scientism which was so marked a feature of the emerging modern world was routinely employed not in the objective search for new truths, but in the determined recycling of the old lies.[28]

The responses to gender and social domination thus far: liberal progressives, Marxists, and romantics, have all failed. Professor Ruether argued that we need a new order in which we rediscover the finitude of earth as a balance of elements that harmonize together to support all life. Then we could see the innerconnectedness of all life, all parts of the creation, each with a role and an importance in an ecological balance. We need a just and livable society.[29]

There is not just one environment, there are many: There is your environment and mine, ours, the built, the natural, the moral, the social, the urban, the rural—all environments of the countless forms of life. There is not one local or personal environment nor is there even one global environment. Gaia, as the spirit of the earth, is a part of but not the whole of environment. The sum of all our environments is not the environment. We need to stop trying to define it.

In contrast, Ash argued that the environments of all our manifold forms of life are metaphors of the impenetrable reality in which each such form is embedded. In this sense, environment is the medium between spirit and matter: or, put conversely, spirit is that without which matter has no meaning, and to speak of environment is to say where spirit is, to give it a home.[30] In Aristotelian terms, environment is where form dwells. Form gives meaning and identity to matter and thus environment links matter to the transcendent. To the extent that Aristotle's form equaled his idea of the soul, we may be describing the environment as the home of the soul.

If this meaning of environment, the home of the spirit, is difficult to grasp, it is because of the centuries of atomization and the search for substance as the only true reality. But meaning depends on context. To study something out of that context is to destroy meaning. Environment is context(s). It could be argued that our culture is sterile because we have substituted the power of knowledge for the wealth of life.

Despite our mental conditioning to define a thing where no things are, if we can accept the possibility that an answer to the emptiness felt by people is to move beyond the world of causation and the limits of our language, then environment, Ash argued, becomes the answer to our search for meaning in a world made meaningless, a spiritual phenomenon that rejects the dualism on which the Western world has been built.[31] Hopefully, it can remain a spiritual phenomenon, shielded from the theology that reifies the world of essence.

To Ash, this spiritual phenomenon rejects centrism as well. Cooperation, like communism, may require small implementations. He believes, with some justification, that only local governments can function with cooperative interaction, and that to think on the level of nation states for the solutions is to put the fox on guard in the hen house.[32] These words should not be necessary, because we already understand, even if Ash did not, that groups are unlikely repositories of ethical values, and altruism is certainly one of them. Only individuals can be altruistic, and to imply anything else is to once again mislead.

Moreover, to speak of group action is to postpone the necessary individual action, and if there is going to be any eco-altruism it had better begin soon. The alternative suggests that humans may no longer be welcome on earth.

In the final analysis, it is not the environments that are so vulnerable, it is people—the very men and women and children who have been the object of this study from the beginning. The human race is still tied down with the unnecessary baggages of original sin, the need to suffer, and the misery of self-loathing that maintains the focus on me, me, me. All this perpetuates the status quo and short-term solutions to long-term problems.

Both Ash and Berry suggested profound changes before we come to a positive and beneficial understanding of our interconnectedness. Is there not an easier or softer way? Apparently not, and it is encouraging to realize that this understanding is becoming better known. U.S. Vice President Al Gore wrote that we have been so seduced by civilization's promise to make our lives more comfortable that we allow synthetic routines of modern life to sooth us in an inauthentic world of our own making. Life is easy; we don't sow, reap, hunt, gather, nor suffer the cold. We can heal sick people, fly through the air, even go under the ice of the North Pole.

> And as our needs and whims are sated, we watch electronic images of nature's destruction, distant famine, and apocalyptic warnings, all with the bone-weariness of the damned. "What can we do?" we ask ourselves, already convinced that the realistic answer is nothing.[33]

With the future so open to doubt, he continued, we routinely choose to indulge our own generation at the expense of everyone who follows. The self is enshrined as the unit of ethical account, separate and distinct not just from the natural world but even from a sense of obligation to others.[34] We have created alienations worse than those described by Hegel and Marx.

As Berry wrote, we don't need a human answer to the earth problem, we need an earth answer. The earth will solve its problems, he wrote, and possibly our own, if we will let the earth function in its own ways. We need only to listen to what the earth is telling us, even though what we hear varies with the shape of our outer ear,[35] just as we need to listen to what our souls tell us we need to do. But this will not happen so long as we are entranced with old answers. Until we have explained this to ourselves, we will never break the spell that has seized us.[36]

What is the spell that has seized us? The spell of that "realism," which denies what it cannot see, denies the fundamental worth of a world that surrounds and sustains us, and denies the cooperation and caring of the earth's nonhuman population. Humans need to become a part of what is already there. An eco-altruism sums up the feeling that in order to receive we must give, and that, in giving, we are acknowledging our great debt to the worlds around us.

We can change. As Maya Angelou said so poetically a few years ago, history need not be lived again.[37] We can learn to stop relying on externals and begin the trip ourselves. We can learn to love—ourselves, our neighbors in need, and our gods, whoever they might be. The alternative is too unpleasant. And, in changing, in loving, we will look in and out and up and down to rediscover that we are connected in many, many lovely ways—in and out of and through the area of silence. And then we will become more a regenerative part of the whole instead of a destructive, self-centered wimp looking for an external savior.

NOTES

1. Janet Macunovich, "Adding Dirt Atop Bulbs is OK if You Take it a Little at a Time," *The Detroit News*, January 31, 1998, p. 14d.

2. Ibid.

3. Ludwig Feuerbach, "Preliminary Theses for a Reform of Philosophy," *Anekdota*, February, 1843.

4. See James R. Ozinga, *The Recurring Dream of Equality* (New York: University Press of America, 1996), Chapter 8, and James R. Ozinga, "The End of Ideology in the Soviet Union," in Michael Urban, ed., *Ideology and System Control in the USSR and Eastern Europe* (London: MacMillan, 1991).

5. Robert P. Ambroggi, "Water," *Scientific American*, vol. 243, 3, September 1980; cited in James R. Ozinga, *The Prodigal Human* (Jefferson, NC: McFarland, 1985), p. 119.

6. Ozinga, ibid.

7. See Richard A. Kerr, "U.S. Weather and the Equatorial Connection," *Science*, 216, 4546, May 1982, pp. 608–610.

8. Ludwig Wittgenstein, *Tractatus Logico-philosophicus*, cited in Donald Palmer, *Looking at Philosophy* (Mountain View, CA: Mayfield, 1988), p. 348.

9. D. O. van Nieuwenhuijze, "Absolutely Relative: The Realization of Reality," *Problems of Values and (In)Variants* (Amsterdam: Thesis Publishers, 1995), pp. 139–148. Special issue of *Systemica*, the Journal of the Systeemgroep Nederland.

10. Keith Reid, *Nature's Network: Interdependence in Nature* (Garden City, NY: Doubleday Natural History Press, 1970), p. 11.

11. Ibid., p. 12. Some would add a Noosphere as a sixth level, referring to the biosphere as altered consciously and unconsciously by human activity.

12. See Charles Darwin, "The Linnean Society Papers," in Philip Appleman, ed., *Darwin: A Norton Critical Edition* (New York: Norton, 1970), p. 83; cited in Robert Augros and George Stanciu, *The New Biology: Discovering the Wisdom in Nature* (Boston: New Science Library, Shambhala Publications), pp. 89, 92; Thomas Huxley, "The Struggle for Existence in Human Society," in *Evolution and Ethics and other Essays* (New York: Appleton, 1896), p. 200; and Robert Ross, ed., *Alfred, Lord Tennyson, In Memoriam* (New York: Norton, 1973), stanza 561, p. 36. Also see Charles Darwin, *Origin of the Species*, Sixth Edition (London: 1872, reprinted New York: Mentor, 1958), p. 74.

13. Robert MacArthur, "Population Ecology of Some Warblers of Northeastern Coniferous Forests," *Ecology*, 39, October 1958, pp. 599, 617.

14. Carl F. Von Weizacker, *The Worldview of Physics*, Marjorie Green, trans. (Chicago: University of Chicago Press, 1952), p. 31; cited in Augros and Stanciu, p. 13.

15. Augros and Stanciu, *The New Biology*, pp. 230–231.

16. Ibid.

17. Gene S. Stuart and George E. Stuart, *Lost Kingdoms of the Maya* (Washington, DC: National Geographic Society, 1993), p. 139.

18. Thomas Berry, *The Dream of the Earth* (San Francosco, CA: Sierra Club Books, 1988), pp. 13–17.

19. Ibid, p. 21.

20. Maurice Ash, *The Fabric of the World: Towards a Philosophy of Environment* (Devon: Green Books, Ford House, Harland Bideford 1992), p. 11.

21. Ibid., pp. 29–30. The notion of a different form of reality is as difficult to explain as Machiavelli's notion of a different kind of morality for the Prince. The problem lies in calling both conventional and princely ethical systems moral, as it is in calling the area of silence "real." The fun part is that one can say that although God does not exist she is nonetheless quite real.

22. Ibid., pp. 33–34.

23. Ibid.

24. Karen Blair, "Cubal Grids: Invariable Civilizational Assumptions, Variable Human Values," paper read at the eighth International Conference on General Systems Theory, Amsterdam, April 1993, p. 3.

25. Ash, p. 44.

26. Donald Palmer, p. 349.

27. R. R. Ruether, *To Change the World: Christology and Cultural Criticism* (New York: Crossroad, 1988), p. 58.

28. Rosalind Miles, *The Women's History of the World* (New York: Harper and Row, 1988), p. 190.

29. Ruether, p. 67.

30. Ash, p. 54.

31. Ibid., p. 59.

32. Ibid., p. 68.

33. Al Gore, *Earth in the Balance: Ecology and the Human Spirit* (New York; Plume Books, 1993), pp. 240–241.

34. Ibid.

35. "Breakthroughs; The Body, What's a Pinna For?" *Discover*, vol. 20, 2, February 1999, p. 24. This short piece reported work accomplished by biophysicist John van Opstal at the University of Nejmegen in the Netherlands.

36. Thomas Berry, p. 35.

37.   Maya Angelou, "On the Pulse of Morning," *The New York Times*, January 21, 1993, p. 10.

Part IV

Conclusion

Still thinking of altruism as doing something for someone else at some cost to oneself, and of selfishness as doing something for oneself at some cost to others, there is one more dimension of altruism that has not yet been considered that is arguably its most important function: destroying the opposition by consuming it entirely.

Examples of one force eating its opposition hardly suggests anything positive. It suggests instead a cannibal society sitting around a campfire watching a huge pot in which the missionary and her husband are contained. Nonetheless positive images do exist. A new medication, herceptin, is a fighter against some aggressive forms of breast cancer, and the manner in which herceptin attacks the cancer cells is said to resemble eating; the herceptin literally eats the cancer, and in the process destroys the opponent and removes it from the field. So this is a situation where the problem is consumed by its opponent rather than moved from one place to another as with a sponge and a wiped up problem.

Chapter 10 describes, therefore, an altruism that consumes its enemy, selfishness. In so doing, virtue is consuming vice; virtue is eating that which pulls us away from God, from others, from ourselves, and removes the vice from the arena. The selfishness is entirely consumed by the altruism.

In order for this to be seen clearly, the notion of original sin needs to be destroyed. It is a strange, mistaken idea that should have never become part of orthodox Christianity.

Chapter 10

Altruism as the Consumer of Sin

Throughout the previous chapters altruism has been discussed in many different ways; as a possible genetic instinct for survival, another way of describing natural law—that ethical sense buried in human consciousness, or as an instinct toward the social and the collective. Additionally, barriers to altruistic development are surprisingly strong—chemical activity in the brain that interferes with the actors' desire for virtuous behavior, religions, and ideologies that organize the ethical spirit right out of an individual, and absolute goals that make altruism seem the exclusive property of saints and never humans. The discussion then wandered into invisible altruism that sometimes goes awry, with invisible hands that apparently only push selfishness, misplaced altruism that can retard progress, and eco-altruism where the connectedness necessary for altruistic behavior is most unclear.

It is time to address a final dimension of altruism that in a way sums up all of the foregoing discussions. Altruism is a virtue, there is no doubt about that, but more than that it seems like altruism is the queen of virtues with power to affect the entire rest of a person's life. Altruism in this instance is the antidote to sin. It is a strong virtue that actually prevents sin at times and even at other times may erase it temporarily from the individual's life. In this instance altruism is a sin-eater, which actually makes it possible to contemplate an hour, or a day, or maybe even a week without sin.

The concept of sin-eater comes from ancient times when, it was believed, there were souls called sin-eaters who acted very much like carrion-eating crows eating the roadkill along the highway. Dr. Clarissa P. Estés described sin-eaters as souls or spirits, birds, or animals, and sometimes humans, who somewhat like a scapegoat, took on the sins, the waste, of the community so people could be redeemed or cleansed. As in Norse mythology,

> the sin-eaters are carrion eaters who devour the
> dead, incubate them in their bellies, and carry
> them to Hel, who is not a place but a person.
> Hel is the Goddess of life and death. She shows
> the dead how to live backward. They become
> younger and younger until they are ready to be
> reborn and re-released back into life.[1]

So they really are cleansed entirely, re-released as innocents, sinless;
having had their sins removed by the altruistic act of sin-eating which has
made them clean again. Sin-eating has a gruesome sense to it, just as vultures
or carrion crows do because they are symbols of death, indicators of carrion
that connotes decay and rot. To tie altruism to such a negative concept would
seem counterintuitive unless it is remembered the crows and the vultures are
nature's clean-up crew, and that altruism too is consuming the carrion, the sin,
and making it disappear. In the relative absence of sin the person and the
community each are freer to act positively, to seek virtue, to seek to live
according to the will of one's personal deity—giving of oneself to fill the
needs of others. Just as the birds dare performing a cleaning service for the
8ecological community, so also altruism cleanses as it performs the function
of removing sin and negating the heresy of original sin.

Although Norse mythology is rich and would reward more extensive
investigation, the purpose of the above citation is very simple: to introduce
the notion of sin-eater and the concept of something that blots up, consumes,
or eats up, the sins of people and reduces or even eliminates the negative,
depressing, alienating lifestyle of so many people.

When dealing with vultures or crows one knows where the carrion
came from, and indeed what it was before it became waste. Where does sin
come from and what is it? These questions are more difficult to answer
because one is on the threshold of theology and theologians rush in with
answers formed centuries ago that no longer make as much sense.

Sin-eating is not atonement, but an absorption of the sin; not at all
like an Old Testament blood sacrifice seeking to atone for one's misdeeds. If
the Bible's Old Testament is correct, blood sacrifices played a large role in
propitiating an often angry Hebrew deity. Atoning sacrifices other than blood
are also possible even if they make as little sense as a blood sacrifice. These
sacrifices would include promises of better conduct or avowals of improvement
that are a bartering with the deity along the lines of "If you will heal my wife
[child, mother, husband] I will become a missionary serving in the most
dangerous part of a major city." This bartering abomination of reciprocal love
is taught by church leaders and it is also in the Bible, so it is no wonder that
people believe that God will not lift a "finger" until they lift an entire hand.

The God in whom they believe does not respond to need, but to bargains, like a caricature of a greedy moneylender, a shylock, in the backroom of a dirty house. This bargain hunter is God? Think of Martin Luther's promise to God that he would become a monk when he was frightened by an electrical storm. "Get me out of this storm and I will become a monk instead of a lawyer."

These long ago activities beg the question: Was (Is) some sort of sacrifice necessary? What is an act of propitiation? An act that pleases the one that is being propitiated, an act that cancels the anger or danger from that source. But what is propitiation? We treat it as though it is the act of the weaker toward the strong, a means of controlling the strong. Smiling at the boss when one would like to grimace can be thought of as propitiation in this sense. But the Latin word on which propitiate is based, *propitius*, means favorable circumstances, auspicious circumstances, kindness or graciousness; or to cause to become favorably inclined, to win or regain the good will of, or to appease or conciliate. Its major synonym is helpful. Underlying the idea of propitiation is kindness, helpfulness, or what we have been discussing as altruism. Altruism is propitiation!

Altruism as sin-eater propitiates or helps by doing something for someone else (some–thing else in the sense of eco-altruism) at some cost to oneself. The act of atonement, the sacrifice, is a symbol of altruism, a raree for the uninformed.

But what is it that requires the atonement? Sin. What is sin? Socrates thought sin was ignorance in part because virtue, the opposite of sin was in his view equated with knowledge. The Platonic Socrates, or the Socrates that is hard to distinguish from Plato in his Dialogues, believed in the power of a dialectical argument to scrape away the encrustation from what one already knew so that the knowledge of the world of the forms could spring free. This knowledge, according to Plato not available to all, was achieved by an intuitive flash near the end of one's education. Those with this knowledge became the philosopher kings or queens in the polis and ruled virtuously over the protectors and the producers. So knowledge was virtue and led to power but not material wealth. Vice or ignorance, on the other hand, was evil.

To religious people who became leaders of church organizations sin was alienation from God caused by human self-will. The purpose of the religion was to bridge that gap between humans and their deity and end the alienation, but instead the reverse happened. Church leaders did more than anyone else to perpetuate and deepen the alienation because in their ignorance they externalized God to the point where the deity was a long way from the human. Since this externalization served the purpose of strengthening the organization even as it weakened the spiritual life of individual church members, it was in the self-interest of church leaders to act just as they did. Such might be an unkind view of the clergy, but perhaps there is some truth to it. The point of the discussion, however, is not the clergy, but the

individual who has less of a sense of God about him or her and more of a
sense of the importance of ritual and church attendance as significant for
salvation. The sense of God within a person may be offensive to some who
believe that their deity is in a single place or cannot be multipresent, as the
theologians put it, because having God in me seems to preclude God being in
heaven where he or she "is supposed to be." The strong emphasis on God in
me is normally associated with mysticism, and the God who is too far away
is usually the companion of a dry orthodoxy in the established church. The
Christian Church has swung from one end of this continuum to the other over
the centuries but usually holds to the dry orthodoxy as tightly as possible.
Mysticism seemed dangerous to church leaders because common people got
involved, just as democracy seemed like anarchism to political tyrants who
feared the masses. British Tories in the late eighteenth century, for example.
German princes in the sixteenth and seventeenth centuries, for another.
Religious leaders since the defeat of the Donatists in North Africa. An
external deity some distance from the believer was thought to be the divine
paradigm of earthly hierarchy. It took German philosophers to begin setting
this record straight.

   Immanuel Kant, for example, argued that our sense of morality, our
sense of goodness does not come from experience, but is part of our inherent
structure. Our moral nature, our sense of goodness and the source of our
altruism is present in every person of every race—an absolute, internal tribunal
commanding us without condition or qualification to do the right thing for its
own sake as an end in itself. The imperative of this sense of morality is
categorical, according to Kant, absolute or without exception. This morality
did not need religion at all because the moral good was innate. For Kant,
therefore, God was not a substance existing outside a person but a moral
relation within. The idea of such a being, before whom all would bend the
knee, and so on, arises out of the categorical imperative, and not vice-versa.
The Supreme Being, he wrote, is a creation of reason, not a substance outside
me.[2] This idea was followed up in a different way in the nineteenth century
by a young Hegelian named Ludwig A. Feuerbach, who argued in his *Essence
of Christianity* that the very idea of an external God alienates us from our own
nature by positioning God as an impossible perfection over against our human
frailty.[3] Feuerbach wrote that we did this to ourselves a long time ago, forgot
that we did it, and foolishly began to worship what we ourselves had created.
This would not have been so troublesome if we had left it alone. But as the
religion became more sophisticated, somebody or many somebodies pushed the
notion of God away even further, making the distance between humans and the
deity so great, so distinct, so other, that people in turn became less and less
like God; like weak children away from their parents. God became a
stranger, an externalized phenomenon in the world of noumena, an infinite to
our finitude, a perfect to our flaws, a joy to our wretchedness, a personified

strength to our puling alienation. As Karen Armstrong wrote, Feuerbach put his finger on an essential weakness in the Western tradition, always perceived as a danger in monotheism. He referred to the kind of projection that pushes God outside the human condition and argued that that could result in the creation of an idol. Other traditions, Armstrong continued, had found various ways of countering this danger, but in the West it was unfortunately true that the idea of God had become increasingly externalized and had contributed to a very negative conception of human nature. Ever since Augustine there has been an emphasis on guilt and sin, struggle and strain in the religion of God in the West, which was alien, for example, to Greek Orthodox theology.[4]

Augustine, who lived from 354 to 430A.D., was an interesting man who lived as a Manachean dualist, deserted his mistress of some fifteen years and his only son to become eventually a part of the Catholic Church hierarchy—ultimately the Bishop of Hippo. It was this man's belief about sin that came to be known as "original sin," a universalized account of his own life visible in his *Confessions.* He felt that he was desperately lost, sick, helpless, adrift with a paralyzed moral will as he awaited the redemptive grace that came through the church and would penetrate his consciousness and effect his salvation. Augustine sounds like a spiritual weakling, a self-pitying wimp, but then any man who deserts his woman and child should suffer a lack of sympathy even if he was later made a saint by some short-sighted people. Pelagius, a British monk that Augustine detested, felt that Augustine's *Confessions* exhibited pious self-indulgence. Pelagius was a strong advocate of free will. It was easy for Augustine to deny free will; it hadn't worked for him and besides anything Pelagius held had to be incorrect. What then was the opposite of free will that Augustine could support? Original sin. And it was Augustine's views that prevailed. He convinced others of the correctness of his dark vision of human nature "ravaged by original sin and overrun by lust for power."[5]

Thus, in trying to discover the meaning of sin the phrase "original sin" has arisen, a concept referring to a universal sinfulness in which all participate. This is a state of sin existing in the human individual prior to any sinful behavior and includes a tendency toward sin and depravity. This original sin, which in Christian theology is held to be inherent in humanity as a direct result of Adam's rebellion in the Garden of Eden is held by many Christians to have resulted in the loss of saving grace. What these words mean is that because Adam sinned, everyone that is born is tainted with that "original" sin. This in turn means that the newborn who is only four minutes old is already a sinner, a very strange concept. When one tries to ascertain how this "sin" of Adam (that we haven't figured out yet) is passed along to everyone one is tempted to think of genes, but advocates of original sin will not go that far. Perhaps this explanation is too scientific. What one is left with is the unsatisfactory feeling that this big deal called original sin is nothing more than the acknowledgment that we are humans and not perfect. Indeed, this is how many religious people define original sin, when they are pushed a little, and it seems innocuous. But it most definitely is not toothless. Original sin buffs, or anyone who reads Augustine, knows how original sin is transmitted—through the sex act. Augustine believed that all people were condemned eternally by God simply because of Adam's "sin." Banished after they had eaten of the taboo tree, Augustine wrote, Adam bound his offspring also with the penalty of death and damnation, that offspring which by sinning he had corrupted in himself, as in a root, and so corrupted all humanity that came later. All human progeny, he wrote, born from Adam and his spouse through carnal concupiscence would drag through the ages the burden of original sin.[6]

What a terrible belief! And how awful it was that other people believed him and made it a central doctrine in Western Christianity. And not just in the past, somewhat darker ages. Original sin continues to be a central doctrine of the Roman Catholic church. In January 1997 an elderly Sri Lanka priest, Father Tissa Balasuriya, was excommunicated for doubting original sin and the immaculate conception of Mary. He also refused to sign a document that categorically denied women ordination as priests.[7] The Pope's action was ridiculous: eternally condemning a man who has devoted his life to the church and its people, theoretically sending to hell one who believes that people do not automatically go to hell. The Church may punish those who disagree, but there is really no defense for original sin. Actually, it makes a great deal more sense to argue that we (both men and women) are born with a natural goodness (the image of God), and we pervert that original goodness with a great deal of assistance from our parents, our schools, our peers, our television, and our leaders's examples. We manage to twist ourselves into selfish individualists who seek for themselves at the expense of others and expect applause for their behavior.

Certainly Augustine's view is possible if one universalizes from a Hitler, a Stalin, or a President Milosevic of Serbia. Thinking of the holocaust during World War II or the starvation of Ukrainian peasants in the 1930s or the raping of thousands of Muslim women by men in the Serb army, one can quite comfortably argue for the depravity of humans instead of their essential goodness. But even though there are negative examples occurring every day, look at the far more numerous decent people around us all the time as well. For example, an emergency room registration clerk at a nearby hospital acts like she never heard of original sin. She buys stuffed animals, coloring books, and crayons, which she passes out to little patients to make them feel better. She's been doing it for eleven years.[8] Doesn't it make more sense to talk of original altruism than creepy original sin?

Centuries after Augustine, Thomas Hobbes justified a strong king by fanning the fear of the masses. Similarly, Augustine used original sin to justify the strong secular government he saw necessary to keep political order and make the world safe for the church. People were so bad, Augustine believed, they needed a strong government to keep them in line. Again, note that the authority and the force is expected to come from the outside. People are treated as though they cannot be responsible for themselves. In the process, again like Hobbes, but also like Martin Luther pulling back from the peasants in 1525, Augustine denied that people possess any capacity whatever for free will. This is where the dour Puritans and Jean Calvin derived their eschatological determinism. Augustine created a definition of liberty that was far kinder to the rich and powerful males[9] with whom he identified than it was to the masses that should have been his Christian concern.

Augustine had an axe to grind, he wanted to justify repressive government, a government the Church could use to enhance its power and organization, and he certainly wanted to justify his desertion of the woman he had lived with for fifteen years. These terrible ideas also suited Jean Calvin, the French reformer partly because he himself was a gloomy, depressed individual. Calvin's need for an authority figure led him to Augustine, and as a result Jean Calvin taught that people were totally depraved. This was wicked nonsense, but from Calvin this horrible doctrine along with ideas of revolution spread to the Netherlands, to the Heugenots in France, to the Presbyterians in Scotland who became eventually the "Roundheads" under Cromwell. These ideas came to the United States with the Puritans and even more so with the influential Shakers. Original sin transmitted by sex, sort of a theological AIDS, led to absurd condemnations of humanity. It led to an unnecessarily strong sense of sin attached to the sex act. It led to a lovely justification for suppressing the female half of the world's population for more than seven hundred years. This neurotic misogyny keeps women out of the pulpits even today. Augustine wrote that "whether it is a wife or a mother it is still Eve the temptress that we must beware of in any woman."[10] Woman's only function was childbearing which passed the contagion of original sin to the next generation, like a venereal disease.[11] How was (is) it transmitted? By the male's semen.[12] Somehow the sin and the guilt got into Adam's semen and this was transmitted to everybody that was ever born except for Jesus, who many believe did not have an earthly father. Presumably Mary's egg was fertilized divinely, and to Augustine that meant without semen. Leaving this aside, what we are dealing with here is the notion that acquired characteristics can be transmitted to future generations, a biological heresy in science called Lamarckism. Stalin promoted these ideas but few others ever did.

The Genesis stories were grist to Augustine's mill. As a result of this "crime" of eating a fruit, Professor Pagels wrote that Augustine said that every man experiences pain, frustration, and hardship in his labor as every woman does in hers: the miseries of human nature now beset both sexes "from infancy to the grave."[13] To Augustine death was not natural, but punishment for that early "sin." Adam's single arbitrary act of will, according to Augustine, rendered all subsequent acts of human will inoperative. Humankind, once harmonious, perfect, and free, now through Adam's choice, was ravaged by mortality and desire. All suffering, from crop failure, wind damage, miscarriage, fever, mudslides, insanity, paralysis, to cancer is evidence of the moral and spiritual deterioration that Eve and Adam introduced. Ever since Augustine, the hereditary transmission of original sin has been the official doctrine of the Catholic Church.[14]

Augustine's notion of original sin was based on his reading of Romans 5 and 7. They are the views of a man who felt deeply alienated from God and who believed that the sacrifice of Jesus propitiated God and atoned for human sins. Paul, the author of the letter to the Romans, was a dualist like Augustine, believing that the mind was godly but the body was sinful. So then, Paul wrote, the law of sin is in my members, fighting with the law of my mind, for with the mind I myself serve the law of God, but with the flesh the law of sin (Romans 7:23,25). Paul believed this, but it was irrelevant. The essence of God becoming human (Jesus Christ) was God reaching out to a people who had wandered away, not a removal of punishment. Perspective is vital; just the slightest maladjustment of one's perspective and the whole idea is twisted out of shape.

The failure to see positively, for example, caused Paul to emphasize the dichotomy between God and people, between soul or mind and body. Body was always bad and the soul or mind always good. This was basic Platonism and it had many applications. For example, if you do not educate females you can claim that they don't have much of a mind. They are therefore, in this odd perspective, much more body-oriented than mind-oriented. Was this why Paul did not want women speaking in church? Why else would this strange idea be accepted when early Christian history was herstory as well?

Similarly, why was the notion of original sin accepted over more commonsensical interpretations that permitted humans to retain some vestige of free will and goodness? The idea that people are basically corrupt demands a strong government and a strong church organization. You cannot do what Adam Smith demanded and let people alone. You have to guide them, trick them, maneuver them into proper channels. So Augustine's ideas were appealing to those who liked strong imperial government and a tightly organized church where orthodoxy was very clearly delineated from heresy.

This was and is original sin. The idea of sin itself seems more difficult to deal with, but this is illusory. What is sin? Ernest Kurtz and Katherine Ketcham wrote that the original meaning of the word sin was a falling away, a falling short that accepts the idea of human imperfection as a given.[15] Human imperfections were not part of the problem; accepting them was part of the solution that involved accepting oneself. Sin was not an automatic acknowledgment of human imperfections, sin was (is) a falling away from virtue. Sin was (is) selfishness, that can be absorbed or eaten by altruism.

This is too simple, one argues. Sin cannot simply be selfishness, it is, after all, a religious concept. Although this has been true, perhaps it is time to pull sin out of religion so that it may be overcome. Leaving it a part of religion dooms any effort to get rid of sin because it is in the interest of the church to maintain it. It is a full employment act for church leaders. Sin made no sense in the beginning of religion's involvement, and it makes no sense to leave it in religion now. Consider how the whole thing began.

All religions seem to have stories about origins, just as does the Judeo-Christian tradition of the world's beginnings in the Garden of Eden, written and preserved in the book of Genesis. This creation story, widely accepted as an alternative to human evolutionary beginnings, placed a man and a woman (Adam and Eve) in a garden that was probably located in a part of the Middle East near Iran. There in the garden these two people lived in innocent happiness.

There is no clue from the Bible as to when this was. Late in the nineteenth century it was assumed that the world was created in 4004 BC because this was the total one achieved by adding up the ages of the patriarchs described in the Bible's Old Testament. This date was still taught in churches and church schools near mid-twentieth century (at least in the churches and schools that I attended), but the explosion of information permitted by carbon dating made paleontologists rather than Bible scholars arbiters of the dates of the prehistoric past.

Present day evidence argues for the earth forming some 4.6 billion years ago, with the simplest life forms evolving abut 3.8 billion years ago, multicellular animals around 570 million years ago, and humans emerging from this past around 150,000 years ago.[16] So when the first humans walked on the earth, it was long ago, and the earth was much older still.[17]

There was no mention of all this in the Genesis account, no mention either of an important institution of contemporary society—private property. There probably wasn't any. Not because it had been destroyed or transcended, but because no one had yet thought of it. This was just the beginning of human relations and human interaction with the environment. In the innocence of Eden, private property would not have fit.

There are two conflicting accounts about how the two people got to the Garden. The first account occurs in the first chapter of Genesis. Male and female were evidently created simultaneously on the sixth day of this creation story, on the same day that animals had been made. Genesis 1:26–27 describes not only the simultaneity of the action, but also the strong likelihood that both genders were created in the image of God. In Verse 27 particularly, the author slips from singular to plural as though the word "man" really meant both genders.

The two new people, Adam and Eve, were then told to do what comes naturally: be fruitful and multiply and replenish the earth. Why the word replenish, implying a repeopling when they were the first people was an unexplained mystery. Nonetheless, there they were, living in harmonious peace with every beast of the earth, fowl of the air, and all the creepy things on and under the ground. Everything was theirs to use as needed, everything in common. Also, everything at this point was positive, it was good. No mention was made of avoiding the fruit of any tree, nor was there any reference to any particular tree. It was a story that seemed to resemble other stories of golden beginnings.

But this was not true of the other creation story in Genesis 2, where a good dose of theology was introduced. The second chapter may have had a different author because so many things were changed. The deity portrayed was a stern God and the relationship between God and people was corresponding- ingly harsher. This second chapter stated that only the male was created by God in the image of God out of the dust and mist. Immediately the reader is confronted with not just the male that God had created but also the trees in the Garden like the tree of life and the tree of the knowledge of good and evil. This is no longer a creation story, but the story of how sin entered the world. That's why the trees are needed up front in the Chapter 2 account. This new man, Adam, was placed in the Garden and was told not to eat of the tree of the knowledge of good and evil because if he did he would surely die in the same day.

Having set this stage, the Genesis 2 author realized that there was no female in the picture with whom Adam could be fruitful. So animals were created, after the human rather than before as in Genesis 1, and the man was asked to name all the animals. The real purpose of Adam's naming activity was so that he could find a mate among the animals. (Genesis 2:20) Somehow, even though the impression was given that creation was complete when the man named Adam was created, it wasn't complete at all and the oversight was incredible: the single human had no reproductive capacity as did the animals Adam named. Presumably the animals were all male and female, and naturally Adam did not find a woman companion because at this point in Genesis 2 a human female wasn't yet there. She wasn't there when the Genesis 2 God told Adam not to eat of a certain tree, either. She didn't yet exist. Since Adam did not find a companion among all the creatures brought before him, the Genesis 2 author remedied this situation by having the deity make a woman out of the rib of the man (Genesis 2: 21–22). Why a rib rather than again use the dust and mist? No one knows, but male chauvinists see the rib story as the first Biblical clue that women are to be subordinate to the male of the species. As James Frazer put it, the author of Genesis 2 hardly hides his contempt for women in the lateness of her creation and that from a part of the many.[18]

Even worse, all the later troubles of the human race were ascribed to Eve's credulity in dealing with the serpent, despite the fact that it was Eve's innocence or naiveté (as well as Adam's) that made the Garden of Eden what it was. The unrealistic implication was that people who have never seen a street should be streetwise.

At any rate, the Genesis 1 or the Genesis 2 couple lived harmoniously with the animal and plant world surrounding them. They had no desire for clothing and had no sense that being naked was anything unusual. In addition, there was no need to work for food, shelter, or happiness. Presumably it was a warm climate because there was no suggestion that clothing was needed for warmth, and the earth provided for human hungers and needs apparently without any effort expended by Adam or Eve just as it did in Ovid's Golden Age. It was Adam's duty to dress and keep the Garden (Genesis 2:15), so there was some activity that could be thought of as work, but it would be work that didn't seem like work to Adam. Nineteenth-twentieth century socialists and communists often spoke like this too. People would work in the future society, but it would be like doing a hobby. In Adam's case one gets the impression that it was easy work because all the animals were as irenic as the two people. Did Eve help with this work? Probably.

The two people probably related sexually in the Garden although there is no specific mention of it. There is no mention of breathing either. It is most likely that somebody had sex because Cain had a wife when he was exiled. Did the sex occur before or after the taboo fruit was consumed? This question would be sheer nosiness if it were not for people like Augustine who thought sex was so evil. So if one guesses that Eve and Adam had relations prefruit one is anti-Augustine. Postfruit would be the opposite. Silly, perhaps, but the account in Genesis is no help. Eve and Adam are expelled from the Garden in the last verse of Chapter 3. In the next verse, the first one of Chapter 4 Adam "knew" his wife and she conceived and gave birth, all in Verse 1 of Chapter 4. Verse 2 of Chapter 4 she does the same for Cain's brother Abel. So the Bible is no help in answering the question. Since Cain came so fast one might feel comfortable arguing for the sex prior to fruit, but if a day can be one thousand years certainly a verse can be a year. Moreover, because Cain was the first baby born to human woman ever, shouldn't there have been more details, more excitement, more confusion? Perhaps these are arguments that support the idea of the author being male, but women can be quite reticent about childbirth, even when they are writing in diaries supposedly to be read only by themselves. This was the case with the pioneer women who crossed the United States in the nineteenth century.[19]

Nor is there a clear idea of how long the two people stayed in the Garden before being forced out. Some scholars have said that Eden lasted a few hours after creation was finished, others say a few weeks, while still others insist on several years.[20] Nor is there a mention of the birth of the woman who became Cain's wife. Whether children were born in the Garden or not is an open question. When Cain was banished or exiled from the area where Adam and Eve lived, the reader discovers that Cain was already married. Strange that it was not recorded. In support of Frazer's contention of the Genesis 2 author's misogyny, the woman Cain married had to have been an unmentioned sister. The Verses 16 and 17 of Genesis Chapter 4 told the story succinctly: When Cain went to the land of Nod he made his wife pregnant with Enoch, and Cain built a city after the name of his son.

What comes across from both the myth of the Golden Age and from the story of the Garden is the overwhelming innocence of the people involved. The lack of clothing, for example, in the Garden story. They didn't even know they were naked. This is still true of children. Even after children learn what nudity is they will still bathe unconcernedly with siblings of the other gender. They are innocents like Adam and Eve were, or as kindergartners appear to be. And not only were they supposed to be innocents in the beginning, Jesus later taught that this was something people should become; like little children—or else entering the Kingdom of Heaven was said to be unlikely (Matt 18:3). The Kingdom was to be made up of people resembling little children (Luke 18:16). It seems strange that Eve (or Adam) should be blamed for trusting the serpent when trusting others is what an innocent child mostly does.

Just as with the Golden Age, or many later examples of communal sharing, the Garden of Eden experience was not as long lasting as one might have hoped. Agostino Inveges (1649) speculated that the Garden of Eden experience lasted for one week; beginning at dawn on Friday March 25 and ended at 4:00PM on Friday April 1.[21] In Ovid's poem about the Golden Age, the suggestion was made that the movement of the gods caused the Golden Age to slip into silver: Saturn was sent to gloomy hell and Jove ruled the world. No real sense of time here. Plato's *Republic* was also vague about time. His ideal political system would endure until the overvaluing of honor as compared with wisdom brought it down, and one moved from philosopher kings and queens to something he called a timocracy. The "perfect" society, in other words, develops a virus and begins to degenerate. Jean Jacques Rousseau's state of nature seemed very similar in that the perfections of the early beginning could not safeguard against emergent private property. Karl Marx, reflecting his Hegelian background, saw the virus or flaw as alienation which emerged in the ancient society when people developed religion as a function of their alienation and allowed the notion of private property to evolve without serious challenge. As a result both religion and private property were institutions that separated people from their own best characteristics. All of this was very similar to the development of alienation described in Genesis 3 as having happened in the Garden of Eden.

One of the trees in the Garden bore fruit that the Genesis 2 creator specified as off limits. This tree was called the tree of the knowledge of good and evil. Pushing a fruited tree back into the creation story seems to be a fairly common thing. A fifth century B.C. vase, for example, shows the serpent-dragon of the Hesperides guarding the Tree of the Golden Apples. The woman involved is Athena, the goddess of wisdom.[22] Actually, the fruit in the Garden wasn't the problem, it was the act of eating it that was evil because it would be an act of disobedience. Seeking the will of God for oneself is virtue. Evil pulls one away from God, separates, creates a gap, and creates alienation or an unnatural separation. This means that church leaders who externalized the deity and contributed to human alienation performed an evil act. So knowledge of good and evil was not the problem; the problem was the experience of alienation brought about by the act of disobedience.

The story was told in such a way as to discredit the serpent or snake that formerly symbolized the Goddess that early people worshipped before male gods took over.[23] The story was also told in such a way as to discredit the female. The serpent spoke to Eve who ate of the fruit, and she in turn talked Adam into taking a bite. This allowed Augustine to state that Eve was the cause of Adam's sin as well as his companion in damnation.[24] If these charges are accepted as true, Eve becomes responsible for her own alienation from God, for Adam's and for the whole human race. This attitude was not unique to Augustine even though he agreed with it. Tertullian, who lived late in the second century, castigated women as evil temptresses and an eternal danger to men. He wrote to women as though communicating a great truth.

> Do you not know that you are each an Eve? The sentence of God on this sex of yours lives in this age: the guilt must of necessity live too. You are the devil's gateway; *you* are the unsealer of that forbidden tree; *you* are the first deserter of the divine law; you are she who persuaded him whom the devil was not valiant enough to attack. You so carelessly destroyed man, God's image. On account of your desert, even the Son of God had to die.[25]

Wow. Note that Tertullian was not referring to a long ago Eve who had, in his judgment, sinned. He refers to all women, as though each was in the Garden of Eden making the decision to follow the advice of the serpent and living without forgiveness since that time. Did Jesus come only for males? Or are Tertullian and Augustine simply like third grade boys on the school playground where young males apparently need to vilify young females? Fortunately these children grow up and change their attitudes, but Tertullian and Augustine grew into adults with these strange, misogynist ways of thinking.

Augustine was puzzled that God should have made females at all. If companionship is what God was after, wouldn't another man have been better?

Could hatred for half of humanity be expressed any more clearly? And we allow such men as these to influence us?

This attitude about women was also visible in the author of Genesis. In the Garden of Eden alienation emerged and there was an immediate loss of innocence: the two humans now knew they were naked, and that they weren't supposed to be. They sought coverings of fig leaves. Curiously, their loss of innocence was described positively as an opening of their eyes (Genesis 3:7), but in the next breath both Adam and Eve were hiding from the Creator because, as Adam said, I was afraid because I was naked (Genesis 3:10). Presumably, he had not as yet put on his apron of fig leaves. God then asked, understandably: Who told you that you were naked? (Genesis 3:11). But innocence, alas, could not be easily regained. The nakedness could be covered but the alienation, the awareness of nakedness, could not. Note that God did not say "So What" when Adam confessed their nakedness. God assumes that Adam has a point in hiding his nakedness. The author of these words thought there was something shameful about naked bodies.[26]

Why would the separation from the deity result in awareness of nakedness? This makes no sense except to someone with a dirty mind. These Garden people have never known clothing, presumably, and it would be like being born in a nudist colony. If you were naughty people like Adam and Eve who took a bite of a fruit forbidden them, why in heaven's name would they ever think of their lack of clothing as a reason to hide from God? Would you be afraid because you were unclothed? Of course not. How would you even know about clothes?

Sometimes this is presented as an awakening of a sense of shame, but what is there in the naked body to cause one to be ashamed? After clothing became common, we can become embarrassed to reveal something designed to be worn under other clothing, but this is taught us as children. Adult embarrassment at nudity is more often directed at uncovering imagined body defects, but if one starts nude, why would one be ashamed? If the author of Genesis was attempting to depress sexual attraction by highlighting the importance of clothing, he or she surely missed the boat because clothing increases sexual attraction. But the people who made this stuff up were people who thought nudity was related to sexual desire, and it was sexual desire described as concupiscence or lust, imagined to be the irrational desire to take pleasure in mere creatures rather than in God. Centuries worth of people have believed celibacy good, worthwhile, instead of unnatural and unhealthy. Celibacy is not a solution it is itself a problem. The whole misunderstanding is based on small minded people who overreacted to the Garden story. Augustine believed that the deity had condemned the entire human race on the basis of the one sin of Adam and Eve. The inherited guilt was passed along to all their descendants by the act of sex, or concupiscence—a pollution of the great sex presumably available before the forbidden fruit was eaten. The irrational pleasure in mere creatures was felt most acutely, Augustine felt, during intercourse when rationality was swamped by passion and emotion and God was forgotten.

This act of love during which the God of love is forgotten is the means by which sin and guilt are transmitted? Nonsense. It would be easier to believe that birds carried the sin and left it on everyone's lawn, or that sin attached to the nitrogen molecules that it surrounds us.

More serious consequences were coming, anyway. The Creator, unhappy that his or her command was disobeyed, acted the tyrant. The deity did not seek to understand why the forbidden fruit was eaten, and did not raise the possibility of reversing the whole sequence. For example, in the spirit of giving a second chance to these two created people, God might have said something like,

> Okay, Adam and Eve, have you learned your lesson? Let's go back to yesterday before this occurred, but your memory will be intact. If you disobey again we will have to discuss harsher consequences. As I mentioned before, one of the consequences is death.

Would not a loving parent say something like that? But no, this deity brought out the big punishing guns right away. No forgiveness, no opportunity to propitiate granted, no time allowed for altruism to eat the sin of disobedience. God cursed the serpent who now had to slither on its belly to get around, cursed the woman with dominance by her husband, with the mense (the "curse"), and with "sorrowful" (painful) childbirth. The man was cursed, but not as much as the woman, with hard work; he would live from now on by the sweat of his brow. Of course rich men did not have to work. Rich women still had painful childbirth, however. Interesting.

Nature was also cursed: Thorns and thistles were now to interfere with human enjoyment and their subjugation of the earth. Death entered the world, presumably for the first time, suggesting that life in the Garden was intended to be eternal. The Tree of Life that gave eternity was not a forbidden tree in the beginning, but after alienation occurred it was; both Adam and Eve were evicted from the Garden to prevent their eating from that tree. Interestingly enough, that Tree of Life shows up again in the book of Revelations as a source of eternity and peace among nations (Rev 22:2). A bit further in that same chapter, a tight connection was made back to the Garden of Eden, because only those who did God's commandments were entitled to eat of the Tree of Life.

The Genesis story, like other ancient stories, very clearly informs the reader that we had something once, a life without toil, without sorrow, in harmony with nature and with others, and a life of innocence that was not intended to end. We had it, and we lost it, and all of our life we remember and try to regain it, but it is a flawed or tainted life that can't solve the problem of alienation from God. If everyone actually practiced Christianity, or presumably other religions, the alienation problem would be solved. Close relationships with God would ensue as people genuinely sought virtue and avoided vice. The visible result would be the Kingdom of God on earth: there would be harmony among people who would think of others as sisters and brothers. Sharing would be a way of life, love would be the dominant motivator, egalitarianism would characterize all human relationships, and peace, joy, and happiness would prevail throughout the world as hunger, disease, and poverty disappeared. This would be what things looked like if all actually practiced Christianity. It would in fact be heaven on earth. How does one practice Christianity? By behaving altruistically: loving, sharing, caring kinds of behavior. The result is that sin is consumed and nothing stands between the person and God.

A lovely example is the volunteer work done in Calcutta at the five missions run by the Missionaries of Charity, until recently run by Mother Teresa.[27] Rita Koselka was one such volunteer and she reported that there were dozens like her waiting to be assigned, some older, some younger, some with medical backgrounds, others who sold real estate—all volunteering for two weeks of hands on experience of doing the work that Mother Teresa and her cohorts did all the time. Rita worked at a hospice, a place for the dying. The volunteers were not necessarily Catholic, nor even religious. What united them was their altruism.

The purpose of the hospice was not to cure but to create a situation in which the person could die with dignity. Rita scrubbed clothing and mattresses, cleaned dishes, served food, hung wet clothing out to dry, and tried to make the patients comfortable, tried to show them that someone cared. Communication was not by language, but by holding hands, by empathy. The patients did not communicate with each other—there are dozens of languages in India. Rita made them as comfortable as she could. She was sorry to leave at the end of two weeks.[28]

There is far more benevolent altruism in the world than we take note of because our news facilities are looking for the opposite. Over and over again the mundane things we do for each other go unreported.[29] Sometimes we think we are all alone, but it isn't true.

A lesson can be taken from Buddhism, where life is seen as a dissatisfied existence searching for an otherworldly goal, rather like a moth being attracted by the impossible, such as the moon or a star. The cause of the dissatisfaction, or alienation, was attachment to things of sense, to things of the material world. Peace was not to be found in the acquisition of things, but in release through the limitation of desire for material things. This release allows an ethical conduct and a serenity that wears down the karma that insists on rebirth, resulting in the breaking of the chain of material life.

Buddhism does not have much use for individualism or materialism.

It is an idealist system in the philosophic sense. Wearing down the karma is the wearing down of that which binds together the interconnected elements or ideas comprising an individual. Obviously, erosion of the force that connects these things allows the dissolution of the individual as the parts fly free of the constraint.

The goal is often called Nirvana, a word that means the going out of fire, especially the fire of greed. Synonyms for nirvana are blessedness, bliss, release, or the other shore. The stress in Buddhism is on ethical conduct and while within the ranks of monks there is equality, there is toleration for the inequality among people in the outside world. The goal of Buddhism is individual salvation not the establishment of the Kingdom of Heaven on earth. Nonetheless the force of the religion/philosophy is on the pursuit of virtue, equality as the ideal, and a condemnation of greed. The love expressed by the early Buddhist was (is) a calm, quiet, unemotional goodwill or kindness toward all the world. Later evolutionary developments in the religion changed some of the religious precepts. For example, the calm love was replaced by a more active loving, which necessitated good works rather than a calm good will toward another.

Other religions tell the same story in a different way. Zoroastrianism, for example, replaces Adam and Eve with a similar pair named Moshya and Moshyana. For many cultures and religions it all began with a bird sitting on an egg.[30] In Mithraism, data drawn from drawings and monuments in chapel caves suggest that Mithras was born from a rock surrounded by snakes, and brought forth a lighted torch symbolizing the sun. He came forth naked, plucked fruit or leaves from a tree, and the next scene shows him clothed. No written records exist, but the beginnings seem similar to the Judeo-Christian tradition. Mithras had the light, lost it, and must regain it by slaying a heavenly bull so that life could exist on earth. At least the Mithraites were spared original sin.

How much simpler to be altruistic, to love one's God, and others insofar as one is able.[31] To have a default position of treating other people with kindness, compassion, and respect. To see in others the image of God they can see in you. To see in nature the interconnections that bind us all together in joy and harmony and peace. Such altruism is a sin-eater. It devours selfishness and greed and cruelty, and begins the long struggle to attain the kingdom of heaven, built on voluntary acts of goodness. They don't have to equal St. Francis of Assisi or Mother Teresa. They can be small and many and, as Wordsworth wrote, result in feelings of unremembered pleasure that have a great impact on a good person's life because they are "little nameless, unremembered acts of kindness and of love."[32]

Such is altruism—the basis of hope.

NOTES

1. Clarissa Pinkola Estés, *Women Who Run With the Wolves: Myths and Stories of the Wild Woman Archetype* (New York: Ballantine, 1992), p. 63.

2. Immanuel Kant, *Opus Postumum,* pp. 316–317, cited in Will Durant and Ariel Durant, *Rousseau and Revolution* (New York: Simon and Schuster, 1967), p. 550.

3. Karen Armstrong, *A History of God* (New York: Alfred A. Knopf, 1994), p. 354.

4. Ibid.

5. Elaine Pagels, *Adam, Eve, and the Serpent* (New York: Random House, 1988), p. 118.

6. Augustine, *Enchyridon*, 26.27, cited in Armstrong, p. 123.

7. Celestine Bohlen, "Heresy Brings Hint of Martyrdom to Sri Lanka Priest," *The New York Times*, January 15, 1997, p. 6.

8. Molly Abraham, "Stuffed Animal Gifts Ease the Fears of the Littlest Patients," *The Detroit Free Press*, February 11, 1998, p. B1.

9. Elaine Pagels, p. 120.

10. Augustine, Letter 243, 10 cited in Karen Armstrong, p. 124.

11. Ibid.

12. Elaine Pagels, pp. 109, 112, 131.

13. Ibid., p. 134.

14. Ibid.

15. Ernest Kurtz and Katherine Ketcham, *The Spirituality of Imperfection: Modern Wisdom from Classic Stories* (New York: Bantum, 1992, p. 149.

16. John Noble Wilford, "Fossils Take Scientists Past Biology's Big Bang," *The New York Times*, February 5, 1998, p. 8.

17. For those who wish to reconcile these long ago dates and the creation story, there is a simple method. The vague meaning of the Hebrew word for day allows the interpretation that one day can cover millions or billions of years. Or the word could refer simply to the 24 hours that is its normal meaning. The longer periods would allow time for the earth to be created long ago with people following some 4 billion years later. Actually, this mild adjustment of the Genesis account was suggested a few generations ago by a Dutch theologian named Abraham Kuyper. A wilder attempt to bring the dating of Genesis and evolutionary science into line asks the reader of Genesis to pause a few billion years between the first and third verses of Genesis 1 during that so-called "chaos" period described in verse 2: when the formless earth was empty and dark, and the Spirit of God moved on the face of the waters.

18. James G. Frazer, *Folklore in the Old Testament: Studies in Comparative Religion, Legend, and Law*, vol. 1 (London: Macmillan, 1919), p. 5.

19. Lillian Schlissel, *Women's Diaries of the Westward Journey* (New York: Schocken, 1982), pp. 108–109.

20. Jean Delumeau, *History of Paradise: The Garden of Eden in Myth and Tradition*, Matthew O'Connell, trans. (New York: Continuum, 1995), p. 181. Evidence from Pseudepigrapha, noncannonical sources, argue that the entire time in Eden was in daylight, and that it was only after being expelled from the Garden that Adam and Eve experienced darkness, which thoroughly scared them. Adam supposedly said to God: "For as long as we were in the garden we neither saw nor even knew what darkness is. She and I were both in one bright light." See Rutherford H. Platt, Jr., ed., *The Forgotten Books of Eden: Lost Books of the Old Testament* (New York: Gramercy, 1980), p. 11.

21. James G. Frazer, pp. 183–184.

22. Buffie Johnson, *Lady of the Beasts: Ancient Images of the Goddess and Her Sacred Animals* (San Francisco, CA: Harper and Row, 1988), 154–156.

23. Monica Sjoo and Barbara Mor, *The Great Cosmic Mother: Rediscovering the Religion of the Earth* (San Francisco, CA: Harper, 1988), p. 125.

24. Augustine, *Enchyridion*, 26.27, cited in Karen Armstrong, p. 123.

25. Karen Armstrong, citing Tertullian, *On Female Dress*, I, i. The Pseudepigapkha was available when Tertullian lived. Perhaps he read and believed the following verse from the fifth chaper of the First Book of Adam and Eve, in which Eve supposedly says: "For I alone caused Thy servant to fall from the garden into this lost estate; from light into this darkness, and from the abode of joy into this prison." Platt, *Folklore in the Old Testament*, p. 11.

26. Actually clothing enhances sexual attractiveness that would be diminished if clothing were removed. Clothing creates the illusion that we do not all look alike. Anti-sex people might consider advocating nudist colonies during the warmer months as a sexual turnoff.

27. Rita Koselka, "Connecting with Humanity; Instead of Skiing the Alps, a Forbes Writer 'Vacationed' at Mother Teresa's Nirmol Hridoy," *Forbes*, vol. 160, 10, November 3, 1997, p. 406.

28. Ibid.

29. Just the opposite occurred in July 1999, when the weekly newsmagazine, *USA Weekend* carried a cover story by Annie Murphy Paul, entitled "Born to be Good?" This story highlighted several examples of altruism by children and adults, acts of giving way beyond the norm. More of this reporting would help.

30. Buffie Johnson, pp. 30–33.

31. Kant thought that loving God was impossible because God was not an object of the senses. Unless, he went on, one meant a *practical love*. Then the commandment to love God and neighbor really meant, he thought, to try living in such a way that both God and the neighbor were pleased. Immanuel Kant, *The Critique of Pure Reason*, p. 326.

32. William Wordsworth, *Lines composed a few miles above Tintern Abbey, on revisiting the banks of the Wye during a tour, July 13, 1798* in John Hayward, ed., *The Oxford Book of Nineteenth Century English Verse* (Oxford: Clarendon Press, 1964), p. 67.

Bibliography

Abraham, Molly, "Stuffed Animal Gifts Ease the Fears of the Littlest
   Patients," *The Detroit Free Press*, February 11, 1998, B1.

Adams, Robert, M., ed., trans. *Utopia* (New York: Norton, 1975).

Ager, Susan,"West Branch Man Gets a Gift of Time," *Detroit Free Press*,
   October 12, 1997, p. F1.

Allee, Warder Clyde, *The Social Life of Animals*, Revised Ed. (Boston: Beacon
   Press, 1951).

Angelou, Maya, "On the Pulse of the Morning," *The New York Times*, January
   21, 1993, p. 10.

Angier, Natalile, "Study Finds Signs of Elusive Pheromones in Humans, *The
   New York Times*, March 12 1998, p. 18.

Ansell, Mary, *A Serious Proposal to the Ladies for the Advancement of their
   True and Greatest Interest* (London: Richard Wilkin at the King's
   Head in St. Paul's Church-yard, 1697).

Archer, Trevor, *Journal of Comparative Physiological Psychology*, vol. 96,
   3, 1982, pp. 491–516.

Armstrong, Karen, *A History of God* (New York: Alfred A. Knopf, 1994).

Ash, Maurice, *The Fabric of the World: Towards a Philosophy of Environment* (Devon: Green Books, Ford House, Harland Bideford, 1992).

Athanassakis, Apostolos, *Hesiod: Theogony, Works and Days, Shield*
   (Baltimore, MA: Johns Hopkins Press, 1983).

Augros, Robert and Stanciu, George, *The New Biology: Discovering the
   Wisdom in Nature* (Boston: New Science Library, Shambhala
   Publications).

Ayers, B. Drummond, Jr., "Town Finds Solace in Act of Heroism," *The New
   York Times*, March 26, 1998, p. 21.

Barker, Ernest, ed., *Social Contract* (London: Oxford University Press,
   1947).

Barker, Jonathan, *Rural Communities Under Stress: Peasant Farmers and the State in Africa* (Cambridge: Cambridge Univerity Press, 1989).

Baumol, William J., and Blinder, Alan S., *Economics: Principles and Policy*, Second Edition (New York: Harcourt Brace Jovanovich, 1982).

Belinskii, Vissarion Grigor'evich, *Selected Philosophical Works* (Moscow: Foreign Languages Publishing House, 1956).

Bennett, John Coleman, ed., *Christian Social Ethics in the Changing World: An Ecumenical Theological Enquiry* (New York: Associated Press, 1966).

Benson, Herbert, "Are You Thinking Yourself Sick," *The Family Circle*, vol. 109, 5, April 2 1996, p. 28.

Bernstein, Eduard, *Evolutionary Socialism*, Edith C. Harvey, trans. (New York: B. W. Huebsch, 1912).

Berry, Sara, "Coping with Confusion: African Farmers Responses to Economic Instability in the 1970s and 1980s," in Thomas M. Callaghy and John Ravenhill, eds., *Hemmed-In: Responses to Africa's Economic Decline* (New York: Columbia University Press, 1993).

Berry, Thomas, *The Dream of the Earth* (San Francisco: Sierra Club Books, 1988).

Billington, James, *The Icon and the Axe* (New York: Alfred A. Knopf, 1966).

Blair, Karen, "Cubal Grids: Invariable Civilizational Assumptions, Variable Human Values, in *Problems of Values and (In)Variants* (Amsterdam: Thesis Publishers, 1995), pp. 22–34. This was a special issue of the *The Journal* of the Systeemgroep Nederland.

Bluhm, William, *Theories of the Political System*, Second Edition (Englewood Cliffs, NJ: Prentice-Hall, 1971).

Bohlen, Celestine, "Heresy Brings Hint of Martyrdom to Sri Lanka Priest," *The New York Times*, January 15, 1997, p. 6.

Brown, Brendan, *The Natural Law Reader* (New York: Oceana Publications, 1960).

Brown GL, Ebert MH, Goyer PF, Jimerson DC, Klein WJ, Bunney WE, and Goodwin FK, "Aggression, Suicide, and Serotonin," *American Journal of Psychiatry*, vol. 139, 6, June 1982, pp. 741–745.

Callaghy, Thomas M. and Ravenhill, John, eds., *Hemmed In: Responses to Africa's Economic Decline* (New York: Columbia University Press, 1993).

Campbell, Donald, "Reintroducing Konrad Lorenz to Psychology," in Richard Evans, ed., *Konrad Lorenz: The Man and His Ideas* (New York: Harcourt Brace Jovanovich, 1975), p. 99.

Caplan, Arthur L., ed., *The Sociobiology Debate: Readings on Ethical and Scientific Issues* (New York: Harper & Row, 1978).

Cicero, *On the Commonwealth*, George H. Sabine and Stanley B. Smith, trans. (New York: Macmillan, 1976).

Cipolla, Carlo, *The Economic History of World Population* (Baltimore, Penguin Books, 1962).

Cohen, Gerald, "The Synaptic Properties of Some Tetrahydroisoquinoline Alkaloids," in *Alcoholism: Clinical and Experimental Research,* vol. 2, 2, April 1978, p. 121.

Crossan, John Dominic, *The Historical Jesus: The Life of a Mediterranean Jewish Peasant* (San Francisco: Harper Collins, 1992).

Crow, James F., "Genes that Violate Mendel's Rules," *Scientific American,* vol. 240, 2, February 1979, pp. 134ff.

Daniel, Carol, "Depressed? Just Pop the Prozac," *The New Statesman,* vol. 126, 4352, September 1997, p. 18.

Daniels, Robert, A., "Nest Guard Replacement in the Anarctic Fish *Harpagifer bispinis*: Possible Altruistic Behavior," *Science,* vol. 205, 4408, August 24, 1979, pp. 831–833.

Darwin, Charles, "The Linnean Society Papers," in Philip Appleman, ed., *Darwin: A Norton Critical Edition* (New York: Norton, 1970).

Darwin, Charles, *Origin of the Species*, Sixth Edition (London: 1872; reprinted New York: Mentor, 1958).

Dawkins, Richard, *The Selfish Gene* (New York: Oxford University Press, 1976).

Dawson, Doyne, *Cities of the Gods: Communist Utopias in Greek Thought* (New York: Oxford University Press, 1962).

DeBlassie, Paul, *Toxic Christianity* (New York: Crossroad, 1992).

DeLue, Steven, *Political Thinking, Political Theory, and Civil Society* (Boston: Allyn and Bacon, 1997).

Delumeau, Jean, *History of Paradise: The Garden of Eden in Myth and Tradition,* Matthew O'Connell, trans. (New York: Continuum, 1995).

deZeeuw, Gerard, "Social change and the design of enquiry," in Felix Geyer and Johannes van der Zouwen, eds., *Sociocybernetic paradoxes: Observation, Control and Evolution of Self-Steering Systems* (London: Sage, 1986).

Dmytryshyn, Basil, *A History of Russia* (Englewood Cliffs: Prentice-Hall, Inc., 1977).

Douglas, Mary and Kaberry, Phyllis M., eds., *Man in Africa* (London: Tavistock, 1969).

Downs, Anthony, *An Economic Theory of Democracy* (New York: Harper & Row, 1989).

Downs, Michael, *James Harrington* (Boston: Twayne Publishers, 1977).

Dunn, John, *Western Political Theory in the Face of the Future* (Cambridge: Cambridge University Press, Canto Edition, 1993).

Durant, Will and Durant, Ariel, *Rousseau and Revolution* (New York: Simon & Schuster, 1967).

Eisler, Riane, *The Chalice and the Blade* (San Francisco: Harper, 1987).

Elgin, Suzette Haden, *Native Tongue* (New York: Daw Books, 1984).

Engel, Barbara Alpern, *Mothers and Daughters: Women of the Intelligentsia in Nineteenth Century Russia* (Cambridge: Cambridge University Press, 1983).

Estés, Clarissa Pinkola, *Women Who Run With the Wolves: Myths and Stories of the Wild Woman Archetype* (New York: Ballantine Books, 1992).

Evans, Richard, *Konrad Lorenz: The Man and His Ideas* (New York: Harcourt Brace Jovanovich, 1975).

Evans-Pritchard, Edward E., *Essays in Social Anthropology* (New York: The Free Press, 1963).

Evans-Pritchard, Edward E., *Social Anthropology* (Glencoe, IL: The Free Press, 1951).

Evans-Pritchard, Edward E., *The Institutions of Primitive Society: A Series of Broadcast Talks* (Glencoe, Ill: The Free Press, 1959).

Ewbank, Thomas, *The World a Workshop or Physical Relations of Man to the Earth* (New York: Appleton, 1855).

Ferkiss, Victor, *The Future of Technological Civilization* (New York: Braziller, 1974).

Feuerbach, Ludwig, "Preliminary Theses for a Reform of Philosophy," *Anecdota*, February, 1843.

Feuerbach, Ludwig, *The Essence of Christianity*, (New York: Harper and Row, 1957).

Feuerbach, Ludwig, *The Essence of Faith According to Luther*, Melvin Cherno, trans. (New York: Harper & Row, 1967).

Fieldhouse, D. K., *Black Africa 1945–1980: Economic Decolonization and Arrested Development* (London: Allen & Unwin, 1986).

Figner, Vera, *Memoirs of a Revolutionist* (New York: Greenwood Press, 1968).

Firth, Raymond, *Economics of the New Zealand Maori* (Wellington, NZ: R. E. Owen, Government Printer, 1959).

Florinsky, Michael T., ed., *McGraw-Hill Encyclopedia of Russia and the Soviet Union* (New York: McGraw-Hill, 1961).

Fragoso, Antonio Batista, "Evangelo y justicia social," *Cuadernos de Marcha*, XVII, September 1968, p. 139.

Frank, S. L., ed., *A Solovyov Anthology*, Natalie Duddington, trans. (New York: Charles Scribner's Sons, 1950).

Frazer, James G., *Folklore in the Old Testament: Studies in Comparative Religion, Legend, and Law*, vol. 1 (London: Macmillan, 1919).

French, Howard W., "Does Sharing Wealth Only Promote Poverty," *The New York Times*, January 14, 1995, p. 4.

Gearheart, Sally Miller, *The Wanderground: Stories of the Hill Women* (Boston: Alyson Publications, 1979).

Gierke, Otto, *Natural Law and the Theory of Society 1500–1800* (Boston: Beacon Press, 1957).

Gilman, Charlotte Perkins, *Herland* (New York: Pantheon Books, 1979).

Glausiusz, Josie, "The Chemistry of Obsession," *Discover*, vol. 17, 6, June 1996, p. 36.

Gore, Al, *Earth in the Balance: Ecology and the Human Spirit* (New York: Plume Books, 1993).

Grant, Michael, *Jesus, An Historian's Review of the Gospels* (New York: Charles Scribner's Sons, 1977).

Griffin, Donald R., *Animal Thinking* (Cambridge, MA: Harvard University Press, 1984).

Gutierrez, Gustavo, *A Theology of Liberation: History, Politics, and Salvation,* Sister Caridad Inda and John Eagleson, trans. and eds. (Maryknoll, NY: Orbis Books, 1973).

Hagood, Margaret Jarman, *Mothers of the South: Portraiture of the White Tenant Farm Woman* (Charlottesville: University of Virginia Press, 1996).

Hamilton, Murray et al., "Identification of an Isoquinoline Alkaloid after Chronic Exposure to Ethanol," *Alcoholism: Clinical and Experimental Research* vol. 2, 2, April 1978, p. 133.

Hamilton, W.D., "The Genetical Theory of Social Behaviour," *Journal of Theoretical Biology*, vol. 7, 1, July 1964, pp. 1–51.

Hammond, Guyton B., *Conscience and its Recovery: From the Frankfurt School to Feminism* (Charlottesville: University of Virginia Press, 1993).

Hanumantha Rao, C. H. *Agricultural Growth, Rural Poverty and Environmental Degradation in India* (Delhi: Oxford University Press 1994).

Hardin, Garrett, "The Tragedy of the Commons," An Adaptation of an Address, *Science*, vol. 162, December 13, 1968, pp. 1243-1248.

Hardin, Garrett, and Baden, John, eds., *Managing the Commons* (San Francisco: Freeman, 1977).

Harrington, James, *The Political Writings*, Charles Blitzer, ed. (New York: Liberal Arts Press, 1955).

Harris, Richard, ed., *The Political Economy of Africa* (New York: Wiley, 1975).

Hebb, Donald O., *A Textbook of Psychology* (Philadelphia: W. B. Saunders, 1958).

Hegel, George W.F., *Philosophy of Right*, T. M. Knox, trans. (London: Oxford University Press, 1942).

Held, Virginia, "Mothering versus Contract," in Jane Mansbridge, ed., *Beyond Self-Interest* (Chicago: University of Chicago Press, 1990).

Hill, Polly, *Migrant Cocoa-Farmers of Southern Ghana* (Cambridge: Cambridge University Press, 1963).

Himmelfarb, Gertrude, *The Idea of Poverty: England in the Early Industrial Age* (New York: Alfred A. Knopf, 1984).

Hoch, Steven L., *Serfdom and Social Control in Russia: Petrovskoe, a Village in Tambov* (Chicago: University of Chicago Press, 1986).

Hoepli, Nancy L., ed., *West Africa Today* (New York: H. W. Wilson, 1971).

Huizinga, Johan, *The Autumn of the Middle Ages*, Rodney J. Payton and Ulrich Mammitzsch, trans. (Chicago: The University of Chicago Press, 1996).

Hume, David, *Treatise of Human Nature* (London: Everyman's Library, 1737).

Huxley, Thomas H., "The Struggle for Existence in Human Society," in *Evolution and Ethics and Other Essays* (New York: Appleton, 1896).

Ibarruri, Dolores, *They Shall Not Pass: The Autobiography of La Pasionaria* (New York: International Publishers, 1966).

Iliffe, John, *The Emergence of African Capitalism* (Minneapolis: University of Minnesota Press, 1983).

Jencks, Christopher, "Varieties of Altruism," in Jane Mansbridge, ed., *Beyond Self-Interest* (Chicago: University of Chicago Press, 1990).

Johnson, Buffie, *"Lady of the Beasts,"* Ancient Images of the Goddess and Her Sacred Animals (San Francisco: Harper, 1988).

Johnson, Roger; Wallwork, Ernest; Green, Clifford; Santmire, H. Paul; and Vanderpool, Harold Y., *Critical Issues in Modern Religion* (Engelwood Cliffs, NJ: Prentice-Hall, 1973).

Kant, Immanuel, *The Critique of Pure Reason, The Critique of Practical Reason and other Etical Treaties, and the Critque of Judgment* published by the University of Chicago in the Great Books tradition. See also *Opus postumum* cited in Will and Auriel Durant, *Rousseau and Revolution* (New York: Simon & Schuster, 1967), p. 550.

Kelman, Steven, "Public Choice and the Public Spirit," *The Public Interest*, Spring 1987.

Kerr, Richard A., "U.S. Weather and the Equatorial Connection," *Science* vol. 216, 4546, pp. 608–610.

Kingsolver, Barbara, *The Poisonwood Bible* (New York: Harper-Collins, 1998).

Kolchin, Peter, *Unfree Labor: American Slavery and Russian Serfdom* (Cambridge, MA: Belknap Press of Harvard University Press, 1987).

Koselka, Rita, "Connecting with Humanity: Instead of Skiing the Alps, A Forbes Writer `Vacationed´ at Mother Teresa's Nirmol Hridoy," *Forbes*, vol. 160, 10, November 3, 1997, p. 406.

Kropotkin, Peter, *Mutual Aid: A Factor in Evolution* (London: William Heinemann, 1915).

Kulikoff, Allan, *The Agrarian Origins of American Capitalism* (Charlottesville: University of Virginia Press, 1992).

Kurtz, Ernest and Ketcham, Katherine, *The Spirituality of Imperfection: Modern Wisdom from Classic Stories* (New York: Bantam, 1992).

Landry, Mim J., "Serontonin and Impulse Dyscontrol: Brain Chemistry Involved in Impulse and Addictive Behavior, *Behavioral Health*

Management, vol. 14, 1, January-February 1994, p. 35.

Lane, Mary E. Bradley, "Mizora: A Prophecy," in Ruby Rohrlich and Elaine Hoffman Baruch, eds., *Women in Search of Utopia* (New York: Schocken Books, 1984).

Lemonick, Michael D., "The Mood Molecule," *Time*, vol. 150, 13, September 9, 1997, pp. 75–82.

Levtzion, Nehemia and Fisher, Humphrey J., *Rural and Urban Islam in West Africa* (Boulder, CO: Lynne Rienner, 1987).

Lewin, Roger, "Predators and Hurricanes Change Ecology," *Science*, vol. 221, 4612, August 5, 1983, pp. 737–740.

Lewin, Roger, "Santa Rosalia Was a Goat," *Science*, vol. 221, 4611, August 12, 1983, pp. 636–639.

Lewontin, Richard C., "Adaptation," *Scientific American*, vol. 239, 3, September 1978, p. 215.

Linnaeus, "Oeconomia Naturae" in Vol 2 of Johann C. D. Screber, ed., *Amoenitates academicae seu dissertationes variae physicae, medicae, botanicae antehac seorsim editae nunc collectae et auctae cum tabulis, aeneis* (Erlangen: J. J. Palm, 1785–1790).

Lowry, Bullitt and Gunter, Elizabeth Ellington, eds. & trans., *The Red Virgin—Memoirs of Louise Michel* (University, AL: University of Alabama Press, 1981).

Luterman, Alison, "Jesus Incognito," *The Sun*, January 1999, p. 28.

MacArthur, Robert, "Population Ecology of Some Warblers of Northeastern Coniferous Forests," *Ecology*, vol. 39, October 1958, pp. 599, 617.

Macunovich, Janet, "Adding Dirt Atop Bulbs is OK if You Take it a Little at a Time," *The Detroit News*, January 31, 1998.

Mair, Lucy, *African Societies* (London: Cambridge University Press, 1974).

Mandeville, Bernard, *The Fable of the Bees* (London, Printed for J. Tonson at Shakespeare's-Head over against Katherine-Street in the Strand, 1733).

Mansbridge, Jane, ed., *Beyond Self-Interest* (Chicago: University of Chicago Press, 1990).

Maritain, Jacques, *The Rights of Man and Natural Law*, Doris C. Anson, trans. (New York: Charles Scribner's Sons, 1943).

Marx, Karl, and Engels, Friedrich, *Marx-Engels Selected Works* (Moscow: Progress Publishers, 1970).

Marx, Karl, *The Poverty of Philosophy* (Moscow: Foreign Languages Publishing House, n.d.).

Masters, Roger D., "Is Sociobiology Reactionary? The Political Implications of Inclusive-Fitness Theory," *The Quarterly Review of Biology*, vol. 57, 3, September 1982, pp. 275–292.

Mayerhof, Milton, *On Caring* (New York: Harper & Row, 1971).

McCormick, Patrick, *Sin as Addiction* (New York: Paulist Press, 1989).

McGovern, Arthur, *Marxism: An American Christian Perspective* (Maryknoll,

NY: Orbis, 1990).

McLellan, *Karl Marx, His Life and Thought* (New York: Harper & Row, 1973).

Meyer, Alfred G., *The Feminism and Socialism of Lily Braun* (Bloomington. Indiana University Press, 1985).

Midgley, Mary, *Beast and Man: The Roots of Human Nature* (Ithaca, NY: Cornell University Press, 1978).

Miles, Rosalind, *The Women's History of the World* (New York: Harper & Row, 1988).

Miller, James, *Living Systems* (New York: McGraw-Hill, 1978).

Milne, L. and Milne, M., "The Social Behavior of Burying Beetles," *Scientific American*, vol. 235, 2, August 1976, pp. 84–89.

Möltmann, Jurgen, *Religion, Revolution, and the Future*, M. Douglas Meeks, trans. (New York: Charles Scribner's Sons, 1969).

Murdock, George Peter, *Africa, Its Peoples and Their Culture History* (New York: McGraw-Hill, 1959).

Myers, R., "Tetrahydroisoquinolines in the Brain: The Basis of an Animal Model of Alcoholism, *Alcoholism: Clinical and Experimental Research*, vol. 2, 2, April 1978, p. 145.

Nafziger, E. Wayne, "Japan's Industrial Development, 1868–1939: Lessons for Sub-Saharan Africa," in Stein, Howard, ed., *Asian Industrialization and Africa: Studies in Policy Alternatives to Structural Adjustment* (New York: St. Martin's Press, 1995).

Nelson, Brian R., *Western Political Thought from Socrates to the Age of Ideology*, Second Edition (Englewood Cliffs, NJ: Prentice-Hall, 1996).

Ortiz, Sutti, ed., *Economic Anthropology, Topics and Theories: Monographs in Economic Anthropology, No. 1* (Lanham, MD: University Press of America, 1983).

Ozinga, James R., "The End of Ideology in the Soviet Union," in Michael Urban, ed., *Ideology and System Change in the USSR and Eastern Europe* (London: MacMillan, 1991).

Ozinga, James R., *The Recurring Dream of Equality: Communal Sharing and Communism Throughout History* (Lanham, MD: University Press of America, 1995).

Ozinga, James R., *The Prodigal Human* (Jefferson, NC: McFarland, 1985).

Pagels, Elaine, *Adam, Eve, and the Serpent* (New York: Random House, 1988).

Palmer, Donald, *Looking at Philosophy* (Mountain View, CA: Mayfield, 1988).

Pinto-Correia, Clara, *The Ovary of Eve: Egg and Sperm and Preformation* (Chicago: University of Chicago Press, 1997).

Platt, Rutherford H., Jr., ed., *The Forgotten Books of Eden: Lost Books of the Old Testament* (New York: Gramercy Books, 1980).

Pouwels, Randall L., *Horn and Crescent: Cultural Change and Traditional Islam on the East African Coast, 800–1900* (Cambridge: Cambridge University Press, 1987).

Putnam, George F., *Russian Alternatives to Marxism: Christian Socialism and Idealistic Liberalism in Twentieth-Century Russia* (Knoxville: University of Tennessee Press, 1977).

Rawls, J., *A Theory of Justice* (London: Oxford University Press, 1971).

Reed, Christopher, *Religion and Revolution in Russia 1900–1912* (New York: Harper & Row, 1980).

Reid, Keith, *Nature's Network: Interdependence in Nature* (Garden City, NY: Doubleday, Natural History Press, 1970).

Ritchie, David, *Natural Rights* (London: George Allen & Unwin, 1894).

Robson, P. and Lury, D. A., eds., *The Economies of Africa* (Evanston, IL: Northwestern University Press, 1969).

Roe, A., and Simpson, G. G., eds., *Behavior and Evolution* (New Haven, CT: Yale University Press, 1958).

Rosberg, Carl G. and Callaghy, Thomas M., eds., *Socialism in Sub-Saharan Africa, A New Assessment* (Berkeley, CA: Institute of International Studies, 1979).

Rose-Ackerman, Susan, "Altruism, Nonprofits, and Economic Theory," *Journal of Economic Literature*, vol. 34, June 1996, p. 701.

Rosenthal, Bernice G., *Dmitri Sergeevich Merezhkovsky and the Silver Age: The Development of a Revolutionary Mentality* (The Hague: Martinus, Nijhoff, 1975).

Ross, Robert, ed., *Alfred, Lord Tennyson, In Memoriam* (New York: Norton, 1973).

Rountree, Helen C. and Davidson, Thomas, *Eastern Shore Indians of Virginia and Maryland* (Charlottesville: University of Virginia Press, 1997).

Ruether, R. R., *To Change the World: Christology and Cultural Criticism* (New York: Crossroad, 1988).

Russell, Bertrand, *Philosophical Essays* (London: George Allen & Unwin, 1966).

Sandys, George, *Ovid's Metamorphosis: Englished, Mythologized and Represented in Figures*, Karl Hulley and Stanley Vandersall, eds. (Lincoln: University of Nebraska Press, 1970).

Schlissel, Lillian, *Women's Diaries of the Westward Journey* (New York: Schocken Books, 1982).

Scott, Sarah, *A Description of Millenium Hall and the Country Adjacent: Together with the Characters of the Inhabitants and such Historical Anecdotes and Reflections, as may excite in the reader Proper Sentiments of Humanity* (London: Printed for J. Newberry at the Bible and Sun, St. Paul's Churchyard, 1767).

Sheehan, Thomas, *The First Coming: How the Kingdom of God Became Christianity* (New York: Random House, 1986).

Sherman, Paul W., "Nepotism and the Evolution of Alarm Calls," *Science*, vol. 197, 4310, September, 1977, pp. 1246–1253.

Simon, Herbert, "Altruism and Economics," *Eastern Economics Journal*, vol. 283, May 1993, pp 159–160.

Sjoo, Monica and Mor, Barbara, *The Great Cosmic Mother: Rediscovering the Religion of the Earth* (San Francisco: Harper, 1988).

Smith, Adam, *An Inquiry into the Nature and Causes of the Wealth of Nations* (Chicago: University of Chicago Press, 1976).

Smith, Adam, *A Theory of Moral Sentiments* (London: Richardson, 1822).

Smith, John Maynard, "Evolution of Behavior," *Scientific American*, vol. 239, 3, September 1978, pp. 176ff.

Snyder, Solomon, "The Brain's Own Opiates," *Chemical Engineering News*, vol. 75, November, 1977, pp. 230ff.

Steinberg, Milton, *Basic Judaism* (New York: Harcourt Brace Jovanovich, 1975).

Stuart, Gene S. and Stuart, George E., *Lost Kingdoms of the Maya* (Washington, DC: National Geographic Society, 1993).

Trimingham, J. Spencer, *Islam in West Africa* (Oxford: Clarendon Press, 1959).

Trivers, Robert, *Social Evolution* (Menlo Park: Benjamin Cummings, 1984).

Trivers, Robert, "The Evolution of Reciprocal Altruism," *Quarterly Review of Biology 1971*, vol 46: 35–57.

van Nieuwenhuijze, D. O., "Absolutely Relative: The Realization of Reality, *Problems of Values and (In)Variants* (Amsterdam: Thesis Publishers, 1995), pp. 139148. Special Issue of *Systemica*, the journal of the Systeemgroep Nederland.

von Weizacker, Carl F., *The World View of Physics*, Marjorie Green, trans. (Chicago: University of Chicago Press, 1952).

Wade, Nicholas, "The Struggle to Decipher Human Genes," *The New York Times*, March 10, 1998, pp. B9–10.

Wagner, Günter, *The Bantu of Western Kenya*, Volume I (London: Oxford University Press, 1949).

Wang, James C. F., *Contemporary Chinese Politics* (Englewood Cliffs, NJ: Prentice-Hall, 1995).

Watkins, Frederick, *Hume: Theory of Politics* (Austin: University of Texas Press, 1953).

Webster, Bayard, "Study Points to 'True Altruism' in Fish," *The New York Times*, September 18, 1979, p. C1.

Weinberg, Robert, quoted in Nicholas Wade, "The Struggle to Decipher Human Genes," *The New York Times*, March 10, 1998, pp. B9–10.

Wilford, John Noble, "Fossils Take Scientists Past Biology's Big Bang," *The New York Times*, February 5, 1998, p. 8.

Wilson, Andrew, ed., *World Scripture: A Comparative Anthology of Sacred Texts* (New York: Paragon House, 1995).

Wilson, Edward O., "Human Decency is Animal," *The New York Times Magazine*, October 12, 1975, pp. 39ff.

Wilson, Edward O., *On Human Nature* (Cambridge, MA: Harvard University Press, 1978).

Wilson, Edward O., *Sociobiology: The New Synthesis* (Cambridge, MA: Harvard University Press, 1975).

Wordsworth, William, *Lines composed a few miles above Tintern Abbey, on revisiting the banks of the Wye during a tour, July 13, 1798*, in John Hayward, ed., *The Oxford Book of Nineteenth Century English Verse* (Oxford: Clarendon Press, 1964).

Worster, Donald, *Nature's Economy* (San Francisco: Sierra Club Books, 1977).

Yanov, Alexander, *The Russian Challenge and the Year 2000*, Iden J. Rosenthal, trans. (New York: Basil Blackwell, 1987).

Young, Crawford, *Ideology and Development in Africa* (New Haven, CT: Yale University Press, 1982).

Yunis, Jorge J., Sawyer, Jeffry R., and Dunham, Kelly, *The New York Times* July 8, 1980, p. C1; excerpted from *Science*.

Zablocki, Benjamin, *The Joyful Community* (Baltimore, MD: Penguin, 1971).

Zorpette, Glenn, "Parrots and Plunder," *Scientific American*, vol. 277, 1, July 1997, p. 24.

Index

About the Author

JAMES R. OZINGA is Professor of Political Science at Oakland University. He has written six books dealing with political philosophy and East-Central European government and politics.